STRONG
TO THE FINISH

BRIAN HUNTER

D1603448

Strong to the Finish

Copyright © 2018 by Brian Hunter

ISBN 978 1-7323135-0-7 (paperback)

ISBN 978-1-7323135-1-4 (E-Book)

DEDICATION

To the orphaned and abandoned children of Mongolia. You are not forgotten; you ARE loved. I would run 10,000 miles for you if I could.

To my family. Thank you for trusting me to lead us across Mongolia. I couldn't have done it without your love and encouragement. Even though I would fuss when you were wrestling in the tent, and I would yell, "Don't touch daddy's legs!" I loved every minute of our time together. I can't wait to see what our next adventure will be.

To the men God has brought into my life. Greg, Pat, Chuck, Lynn, Mike, and Ron, you have been shining examples of authentic manhood, and I carry your lessons in my heart every day as I try my best to live out the lessons you taught me.

To my Father God. You have been the best dad a boy could ever ask for. Come on; let's go for a run.

TABLE OF CONTENTS

í

ACKNOWLEDGMENTS

I'd like to thank everyone who made this book possible. I'd like to especially thank John Mason of Insight Publishing for his knowledge and assistance, and also my editor, Joshua Lease of Aegis Editing, with whom I had great chemistry.

CHAPTER 1

RUNNING ON EMPTY

Run when you can.
Walk if you have to.
Crawl if you must.
Just never give up.
                                   – Dean Karnazes

"I can't do more miles."

I was in a crisis in the middle of Mongolia. My body was breaking down, the toll too much.

I simply couldn't do it . . .

I couldn't cover the miles necessary for us to make it across Mongolia before the brutal winter hit—not to mention that we'd miss all our scheduled flights out of the country, and we wouldn't be able to afford paying the support team past the deadline.

The expedition had a tight timeframe based on the idea that I would cover more than a marathon, thirty miles, *every day*, six days a week.

Crazy? Tell me about it!

And that wasn't happening. I hadn't been able to find a rhythm—and it was going to destroy our objective across Mongolia.

We were three weeks in, and I was paying the price. We'd change camp every few days, and I shuttled back and forth in one of the support vehicles to pick up where I left off. Every day we wasted crucial daylight hours I could be running to take me back to where I had left off the day before. Worse, this "road" across Mongolia could scarcely be called that. It was a braided weave of washed-out dirt and two-tracks made by the tires of vehicles charging across the Mongolian steppes. I often started my miles nearly carsick from being battered by the pace across the rough roads.

I simply couldn't do it anymore. I couldn't do more miles under these conditions. Something had to give—and it looked like it was going to be me.

It gets worse.

We were out of water. Most of us in the industrialized world have no idea what that really means—we say that when we're out of bottled water and need to go to the store. But most of Mongolia is just one notch above a desert; the steppes are expansive, arid flatlands with sparse vegetation. The plains extend as far as the eye can see in every direction—endless horizons where the massive dome of the sky is brilliant blue during the day and reveals the entire, star-studded Milky Way at night.

It's beautiful, but it's hostile. There's not much drinking water, and when we were *out of water*, we were in serious trouble.

We were there now. I was dehydrated after a day's miles, my body having sweat out perhaps five pounds of water a day that needed to be replaced before the next day's run, leaving me weak and exhausted. My tongue was thick in my mouth, my limbs leaden from more than just a day's run of twenty-five miles.

If I didn't get water soon, I wouldn't be able to go tomorrow. You can't run without water—period. A car won't start if it's out of gas, and a body (which is roughly seventy-percent water) won't run either if it's dehydrated. If we didn't find a way to rehydrate, we'd lose a day's progress, and we were already getting dangerously off schedule.

The expedition was balanced on the edge of a knife; if we strayed just a little bit, it would fail.

It didn't look good. My miles done, we drove on and on and *on* in search of drinkable water. Every hour took us farther from where I left off running—hours we'd have to make up before I could start running the next day. Slowly, the glowing golden orb of the sun sank behind the horizon, painting us with the dying red glow of another picturesque Mongolian sunset, and leaving us in the dark—still with no hope of water.

And with that dying hope of finding the most precious, most basic commodity, drinkable water, I felt my confidence for the whole trip dying as well.

I didn't know how we'd make it, how I could possibly go on.

I wasn't out here on a whim. I felt I'd been *called* to do this. So what was wrong? If this were really for a higher purpose, where was the support, the divine hand of providence . . . the *water*?

Thousands of children, Mongolian orphans forgotten by their families and their government, needed me to find a way. We'd made promises, raised money by saying we could do this. And now, simply because we couldn't find the most prevalent resource on the planet, it could all come apart. Would I be strong to the finish?

Perhaps you've experienced something like this. Perhaps you've launched out into something you felt you were *called* to do—only to slam into a crisis that rocks your conviction and your confidence that you can do it at all. Maybe you feel you're supposed to do something, that you have something higher urging you to step out and try to accomplish a dream that seems unlikely, frightening . . . and wonderful.

Whether you're familiar with the sobering nature of a crisis threatening to destroy your dream, or you're just thinking about launching out into something wonderfully frightening that's bigger than yourself, I have a hope. My hope is that in reading about what we went through, you'll learn something about yourself.

In the summer of 2013, I set out to run fifteen hundred miles across the flat near-desert landscape of Mongolia to raise awareness and money for the orphaned children of Ulaanbaatar, the capital of Mongolia. I did it for them. But I also did it because I felt I was being called to do so, and I had to take a series of small steps of faith that would either lead me to successfully run across an entire country, or would leave me broken, cracked, and thirsty on the Mongolian steppes.

But this book isn't about me. In a way, it isn't even about the orphans, or my steps of faith.

It's about you. I wanted to capture the most important life lessons I learned from this whole expedition and share them with you in this book. Reading it and applying the lessons to your life will save you eight-to-ten pairs of running shoes and some *really* sore muscles.

This book is also about discovering *your* Mongolia—that thing that's bigger than you that you're called to do. It's waiting for you right now, just beyond the horizon. Let's go!

CHAPTER 2

LONG-DISTANCE CALL

People who are crazy enough to think they can change the world usually do.

– Steve Jobs

Before the hundreds and hundreds of miles running, and even before the (not as meticulous as you'd think) planning, what I had was an idea. It would later take on more life and become a calling, but for a time, running across Mongolia was more like a bizarre daydream than anything. I toyed with the idea for about two years before taking any steps to make it happen, and for all that time, the idea of trying to run all the way across Mongolia simply simmered in my heart like dinner in a slow cooker.

Before that crisis moment on the steppes, when we were out of water and unsure how we'd get back on track, a whole adventure played out just getting us to Mongolia.

THE FIFTEEN-HUNDRED-MILE CALL

Run fifteen hundred miles? I'd never run so much as a marathon, but I felt like something was drawing me to *run across Mongolia*.

I did some rough numbers in my head: averaging thirty miles a day, running six days a week and resting one day a week, it would take nearly sixty days to cover the distance.

A guy who had never run a marathon—had never been much of a runner at all—was considering running over a marathon *a day* for roughly two months straight. It was completely unrealistic, outlandish, and ridiculous. No, it was nothing short of *insane*.

Now, I'd read about people crossing incredible distances because they had to. I'd read a book, *The Long Walk*, where six men crossed the bulk of Asia trying to escape the Siberian internment camps in 1940.

I had nothing so concrete driving me. There was no gun to my head or threat to my liberty urging me on.

My thoughts about running across Mongolia were all because of a *feeling*, a prompting. But it was not a passing whim—not the kind I had come up with in the past when encouraged by the wrong sort of friends to try something foolish and manly that started with the words, "Hey, watch this . . . ." I'd been considering this epic trek for about two years, mulling it over, deciding I was certifiable for even thinking about it, putting it away, and then taking it out and re-examining it all over again.

It was either a higher calling from God, or I was going totally nuts.

"Fifteen-hundred miles. The summer of '13." That's what I

had—a distance and a timeframe.

I also had a choice. I could choose to accept that what I felt called to do seemed humanly impossible—and try it anyway. Or I could call it what it was—crazy—and forget about it. The problem was that, in a way, it was never really much of a choice. You see, I am confident that my life had been bringing me along, a step at a time, to a point where I would say *yes* when it was time to do something *big*. Enormous. Foolishly. Crazy, insane, and impossible.

But the journey of a thousand miles—or fifteen hundred—starts with a single step, and *everything big starts with something small*. So I decided that I'd take the most crucial and imposing one of all: I would tell my wife what I felt God was inviting us to do.

You'll notice I said *us* not *me*. That's because the craziest part of all wasn't that I was going to ask her to give me her blessings for a two-month outreach trip to Mongolia, during which I'd run the width of the continent. No, the craziest part was that I was going to tell her I thought *she* was supposed to come too.

Oh, and did I mention that we would bring our kids as well? Like I said, *crazy*.

NO FEAR

If you picked up this book and you've kept reading so far, you can probably guess that the utter insanity of running across Mongolia and taking my family with me actually worked out somehow. We wouldn't do a book about a big failure, would we?

No, you're reading this book because we took one step at a time—until we'd crossed the entire country of Mongolia. We did it, and we survived. So obviously it wasn't as insane as it sounded when I first talked to Lissa, my wife, about it in the summer of 2012.

So rather than belabor the point any more than I already have,

I'd like to start out with a couple of assertions that might surprise you. The first is this: before embarking on the run, in my training I only did one marathon and averaged about thirty miles a week.

The second is that I feel like in some way Lissa and I were *born* to do what God had called us to do—like we'd been prepared by life's challenges and adversities with exactly what we needed to pull this off.

But the key aspect of what let us do this was an understanding Lissa and I shared that you might not hear talked about too much these days. The old timers called it "the fear of the Lord." And if you're not familiar with it, I'd like to take just a few moments to give you a window through which to view the conviction we had.

We were convinced that doing what God was inspiring us to do, no matter what, was more important than literally anything else. We were utterly convinced that no matter how many reasonable and convincing arguments stacked up on one side of the scale for *not* running across Mongolia, the one thing on the other side outclassed them all.

I can see it all in my head—a boxing ring featuring fighters straight out of the children's stories of David and Goliath:

In one corner, wearing the green trunks and looking like an angry thousand-pound gorilla, every rational thought we could come up with—the limits of the human body, the fact that we both had jobs, the welfare of our children, doctors telling me it was impossible, people begging us not to do it, and the fact that it was going to cost us our jobs.

In the other corner, wearing the blue shorts and built like a Jewish carpenter, the fear of the Lord.

The funny thing is, it wasn't even much of a fight.

Rational thinking and every reasonable argument people threw at us wasn't enough to even challenge the respect we had for what God was telling us to do.

RESPECT BRINGS JOY

Explaining the fear of the Lord can be a tricky thing. Most people get the wrong idea when they hear "the fear of the Lord." They think of an old man in a white robe with a grey beard who has arms that look like He has been doing CrossFit® all day. He's holding a lightning bolt poised to fling down to earth at anyone He catches being a sinner.

I get it. I understand why you might have that idea of God. We have seen Him portrayed that way in Renaissance paintings, and the very phrase "fear of the Lord" sounds a bit scary. But, let me explain what I'm talking about in a way that might make a little more sense to you.

When I was younger, I played soccer for a coach that I will never forget. He was hard on me, and he held me to a really high standard. At first I resented his focus on me. I felt like he was treating me unfairly, and I hated all the running he made me do. But it was hard not to like him because he was always so encouraging, and he always praised me for anything I did right.

Gradually I began to see that he pushed me because he saw something in me, something that I couldn't see in myself—potential. He cared enough to want the very best out of me. I noticed that my heart changed towards him, and I began to *want to* perform my very best for him. I hated messing up on the field because it brought me joy to please him. The harder I worked, the more I loved soccer and the more I liked my coach.

Even though I liked my coach, I was scared to death of him. When he had to drop the hammer on the team for sloppy playing, I wanted to climb in my soccer bag and hide. It wasn't because he was mean or even angry. I was afraid because I so disliked the feeling of disappointing him that it would twist my stomach into knots and make me want to try ten times harder at practice.

I respected my coach and wanted to make him happy. That's how I would describe the fear of the Lord—deep awe and respect for God. It brings joy to me to live a life that pleases Him because I know that He believes in me and wants the very best for my life.

FEAR AND FOOLISHNESS

The phrase "the fear of the Lord" is throughout the Old Testament, but Solomon, the wisest man who ever lived, penned what may be the most famous quote: *"The fear of the Lord is the beginning of knowledge, but fools despise wisdom and instruction."*[1] But he was not talking about *human* wisdom and knowledge.

This fear-of-the-Lord concept is the beginning of another kind of wisdom.

I'm going to let you in on a secret you may not know yet if you're new to this whole "faith" business: *God's ways don't always make sense. They're not rational or sensible*, at least, not in our normal human idea of what's sensible.

Paul, who wrote most of the New Testament and is widely considered one of the wisest men of his era, tackled this issue as well when he wrote, *"The message of the cross is foolish to those who are headed for destruction! But we who are being saved know it is the very power of God. As the Scriptures say, 'I will destroy the wisdom of the wise and discard the intelligence of the intelligent.'"*[2]

So where does this leave the philosophers, the scholars, and the world's brilliant debaters? God has made the wisdom of this world look downright *foolish*. Everyone said that our call across Mongolia

---

1   Proverbs 1:7
2   1 Corinthians 1:18-19 NLT

was foolishness, but instead, all of those predictions of doom proved to be foolish.

Lissa and I bought into this idea of wisdom and foolishness from early on in our marriage and in our faith. But before you start thinking that we're special or different, I want to get across to you two things that seem almost mutually exclusive. I already said that before leaving for Mongolia, I was just an ordinary guy—I was not an ultra-marathon, long-distance, cross-country runner. I had no vast wealth of training or experience to fall back on, and I am only a marginal athlete in general. Physically, I'm just an ordinary guy.

The second thing I want you to understand is that *spiritually* I have been groomed since birth, since conception, to do exactly what I did. Everything that has happened in my life prepared me for the challenge God gave me.

Do you want to know something crazy? The same is true for you!

You may not feel like you have any special qualifications or abilities, the appropriate education or training, or even the basic physical or mental prerequisites for whatever it is that you're supposed to do. And you're exactly right. If you were totally equipped with all the muscles and training and preparation when you tackled the impossible, and against all odds you came out on top, then you would think it was *you*. You would think that it was *your* hard work, sweat, smarts, and tenacity that carried the day.

But that isn't what God is interested in at all. That is why He calls those of us who feel woefully under-equipped and ill-prepared: we are totally dependent on Him.

Yet, I am confident that if you look back on your life after having accomplished something impossible, you will see that somehow, some way, God's unique preparation process was actually working all the events of your life for your good. With a kind of wisdom that only makes sense to Him, God was crafting and bending and reshaping your life to get you ready *spiritually* for His calling on your life.

The smartest people in the world may say that what God has called you to is foolishness, impossible, and crazy. But God says, "*I built you for this.*" Through all the seemingly random twists and turns in your life, God has been working, working, working—behind the scenes and in unexpected ways—to bring you to exactly where you need to be along the course that would equip you to be the vessel that He needs at that exact moment.

God has a special call on each one of our lives. My goal is that as you read this book, you will become convinced of His call on *your* life and be encouraged that if I can do the impossible and run across Mongolia because God called me to do it, you can do whatever you feel He is urging you to do as well.

The question I want you to be asking yourself going forward is, "What is my 'Mongolia?'" What is in your heart that God's inviting you to do, yet it seems outrageous and impossible? That is your "Mongolia."

It might be freedom from an addiction, life in a dead marriage, or salvation for your crazy family members. It could be anything—starting a business, or launching your own expedition—just remember, when you partner with God to accomplish the impossible, you're going to find that He likes making the world a better place by helping people. That can have an infinite variety of options, but I have a deep conviction that helping people is the noblest expenditure of our lives. Helping people have better lives makes the planet a better place for *all* of us to live.

Now I want you to think of one other thing: If you accomplished your Mongolia—that impossible dream God has cooked up for you—

would you think that there's *anything* too hard for Him? On the other side of your Mongolia, God has something waiting for you.

BE DANGEROUS

When you have done the impossible because God orchestrated it, you become someone—something—different.

Dangerous.

Those who have done the impossible because of the call of God on their lives become dangerous people. Why? Because you can never again tell them that something cannot be done. You can never again make them believe their God is too small, their problem is too big, or their world too harsh. Someone who has discarded the wisdom of this world for the "foolishness" of the fear of the Lord, who has been used to do the impossible, is by definition one of the most dangerous people alive.

Forgive me here if this sounds like a brag; it's not. I'm certainly not Chuck Norris—my hands and feet are not deadly weapons. But something in my spirit and in Lissa's and in anyone who has stepped out with great faith in God is very dangerous indeed . . . to the forces of evil.

And in the spirit of bragging, let me do a little in the style of Paul by boasting in my weaknesses. Because, before you think that I was able to do what God told me to do because of some sort of unfair advantage, I'd like to brag on my origins. Conceived in Mexico City, my father abandoned us when I was two. I don't remember him. My mom, a single mother my entire life, raised me by herself mostly in Texas. I'm not the product of three generations of godly preachers, and no angels prophesied my birth.

Before running across Mongolia, I was nothing special. Actually, I'm still not! But I am one thing—something that I want to explore in this book and convince you that you can be as well.

I'm *dangerous*.

And when you buy into trusting God and say yes to your Mongolia, you will be as well.

Come with me as we take our first steps across a country fifteen-hundred miles long.

CHAPTER 3

The Beginning of Me

May your trails be crooked, winding, lonesome, dangerous,
leading to the most amazing view.
– Edward Abbey

My dad left when I was two years old. Nobody should ever be abandoned.

Tracing my journey across Mongolia has to go back to the very beginning, which I suppose is the beginning of me.

I was born in 1974 in Guadalajara, Mexico, to American parents working in Mexico City. They got married and shortly afterwards had me. We lived in Mexico City for about two years until my father left, by which I mean disappeared. He was older, and I later learned that he had already tried a family once before he met my mom. In any case, he apparently decided he didn't want anything more to do with us, so he took off.

My mom moved us back to Waco, Texas, where her family lived, and we lived with my grandmother from the time I was very little up through fourth grade. We lived out in the country, but my mom and I both had bad allergy problems. We were sick all the time, so I missed a lot of school.

I think our health troubles were one of the driving factors that urged my mom to make a very brave decision: she moved us to the mountains of Colorado to get away from the Texas allergies and rural, small-town mentality. I'll forever be grateful to my mom for doing this because it really opened up a whole new world for me.

I started fifth grade in Boulder, Colorado, and to this day I can remember seeing the mountains for the first time. It was like coming up from the deep end of the pool and getting the most delicious, giant breath of air. The mountains called irresistibly to me, and from sixth grade through the end of high school, I scampered around on them every chance I got. Day hikes, bouldering, mountain biking—you name it, I loved it.

In eighth grade, my English teacher, Gordon Grant, introduced me to rock climbing. He was a huge rock climber from North Carolina, and he would take the eighth-grade boys on rock-climbing trips. These trips simply blew this little Texas boy away. I fell completely in love with it, and while in high school, I met a guy named Ben Marshall, who became a very good buddy. We got in lots of trouble in school and had some amazing adventures in the mountains on the weekends. The mountains were my life.

Not too many people know that in 1974, I contracted polio, which surprises a lot of people because it's been eradicated in the United States for a very long time. What people don't know is that I was born in Mexico and didn't get the right vaccinations. I only have flashes of memories of being very little and going to doctors' offices for braces and shoes and things, and my mom made sure that I got the treatment necessary to get better. Let me just tell you; if polio can't stop you, you're off to a good start.

I talk about not being special, about running across Mongolia even though I'm an ordinary guy, and perhaps I neglect to mention some internal drive and determination that I received from my mom and from things like battling polio. Whatever the case, I have never liked circumstances to get me down—even when common sense should have changed the course of my actions.

SOLO CAMPING

Like I said, the mountains became my life, and at the tender age of thirteen, I went on my first solo backpacking trip. I was incredibly excited about it and had bought all the gear I would need. I had my external frame pack, a big sleeping bag, a camp stove, and a small tent. I somehow convinced my mom to drop me off on the eastern slope of the Indian Peaks Wilderness. The plan was that she would pick me up in three days after I had hiked over Fourth of July pass and down the western slope of the Continental Divide.

I don't remember my mom putting up too much of a fight; maybe she just trusted me that much. As a parent myself now, I cannot fathom letting my kids spend three days alone, hiking over the Continental Divide—let alone as a single parent like my mom. But she let me go on the backpacking trip of a lifetime, trusting a rowdy, rebellious, and unruly (barely) teenager with all the dangers of a hike of that magnitude.

For me, the mountains were a healthy outlet. The alternative was to be a hooligan or punk, either of which statistics say I was likely to become as a male raised by a single mom.

So that's how I found myself in the Indian Peaks Wilderness on Forest Service land when you could still bring your dog. So I wasn't completely solo; I had Pumpkin the fat Golden Retriever with me. I can remember my mom making sure I had everything I needed at the trailhead before I set out, and my memories of tromping off into the forest with Pumpkin at my side are still very clear.

The first night we got up to the tree line, elevation about 11,000 feet. I set up my light-blue, one-man backpacking tent, made a meal, and asked Pumpkin if she had any thoughts about the USGS Forest Service map or topography. I made us a dinner of beans and rice and washed it down with lemon tea that my mom had packed for me.

I was thrilled to be on such an adventure. I wasn't scared, concerned, or frightened. I was just hungry for challenge and adventure!

The next day, I hiked up over the pass—at least 13,000 feet—way above the tree line. I made it down the other side and just to the edge of the tree line before camping my second night. Here is where you may want to question my judgment, as an early fall snowstorm came in from out of nowhere that night.

Pumpkin and I huddled in my tent overnight as the storm dumped six inches of fresh powder on us. I had to wake up the next morning and push an avalanche of snow off the roof of my tent. I had accidentally left my boots outside, a mistake I only made once. After a breakfast of cereal and brown sugar with powdered milk, I packed up everything wet and started hiking down. Let me tell you, I was glad it was only a three-day trip.

My mom was waiting for me at the trailhead, and I don't think she had ever been more glad to see me in her life. She was pale with worry, but I had a grin on my face from ear to ear. I had braved the mountains and taken (what I thought was) their best shot. I observed a solemn ceremony that has stuck with me ever since.

"Once again we have cheated death and lived to tell the tale," I told Pumpkin. I shook her paw, and we hopped in the car to head home.

I probably needed challenges like this to keep me from going crazy and getting kicked out of school. In a way, the mountains were a type of parent to me: mountains have boundaries; I cannot cheat a mountain; I may get lucky once or twice and get by with something dumb, but if I kept it up, the mountains would smack me down; the mountains are always stronger than I am, and by challenging them, I learned a lot about myself, a lot about taking risks and pushing the boundaries of exploration.

The experiences in Colorado's mountains during my youth planted seeds of exploration in me and told me that I could push myself past what I thought I could do. I tested myself against those mountains, which was good, because other mountains would test me later in life.

However, the mountains could not answer the deep questions of my soul. They had no capacity to fill the void in my heart. The mountains had given me so much that I thought they could eventually fill every broken part of my life. I thought it was just a matter of stuffing enough of the mountains in there.

But here was the problem; there was no mountain big enough to fill that void. No matter how much I climbed, skied, mountain biked, or ice climbed, I couldn't find peace for my restlessness. They couldn't heal the wound from not having a father; they couldn't tell me how to become a man. They couldn't wipe away the guilt and shame of my sin.

It took me a long time to discover that is not the purpose of mountains.

The truth is, in and of themselves they have no capacity to heal or bring peace or save anyone's soul. Now, many people would disagree with me on this point, but the truth is, at best the mountains can be a signpost pointing to the true source of peace and healing. At worst, the mountains are an anesthetic, an opiate, to dull the pain.

The mountains may make a person feel good for a while, but when the adrenaline wears off and the blisters heal, the brokenness, loneliness, and pain resurface. Then the law of diminishing returns kicks in, causing a person to look for longer routes, steeper lines to ski, and bigger mountains to climb in order to get the same temporary relief.

I often find some people have a few misconceptions about running and mountains, so let me take a few moments to tell you what they *won't* do.

I spent a lot of time around runners and fanatical athletes while training, and I have noticed that some people try to use accomplishments as a means of solving their problems. While it's true that exercise has a proven value in reducing stress and other positive physical, mental, and emotional benefits, simply accomplishing things like doing a race doesn't solve our problems. Running across Mongolia did not solve my problems. I have found that people who use accomplishments to try to solve their problems soon discover that after they have gone the distance, have the t-shirt, and the glow of the runner's high has faded, the same old baggage is waiting to take centerstage back over from whatever they just accomplished.

It's then easy to draw an incorrect conclusion that since you still have problems, you didn't do enough—you think you didn't run far enough, push yourself hard enough, or climbed high enough. So it's time to set another goal. It's time to aim higher! The thing is, accomplishing a goal, even a noble one, won't save you. Climbing a beautiful mountain won't solve your problems.

Even doing something great for God, even fulfilling an impossible dream, won't heal or satisfy deep hurts or longings within our souls. Only God Himself can do that.

If you're looking for the fulfillment of your dream to complete something that's missing in your life, you may be waiting a while. I have a lot of things missing from my life — my dad left when I was only two-years old, my mom raised me while living barely above the poverty level, and I was never a burly, intimidating man or dominant sports figure. And as I reached the finish line of my fifteen-hundred mile odyssey, I realized that running across the country had not made up for anything missing in my life.

Mountains, running, hiking, camping, skiing, and all the rest don't have the capacity to fulfill that emptiness—even for a good cause. No matter what method or action God uses to accomplish the dream He has for your life, fulfilling the details of the contract does not have the capacity to fill up emptiness in your heart. If you're looking for a goal to fill up the hole inside of you, you will always be searching for a bigger goal. And while accomplishing the impossible for God may make you *dangerous* and able to believe for any goal, living life to go from goal to goal will just be putting your ladder against the wrong building yet not realizing it until you make it to the top.

Succeeding at a good dream does not undo bad or misguided works. It would be great if life really worked that way, but being the first person in history to run across Mongolia certainly didn't undo any of my past failures. Raising tens of thousands of dollars for orphaned and vulnerable children was great for the kids, but it didn't overwrite or delete the wrongs that I have done in my past.

If you have darkness in your past, setting your sights on some momentous accomplishment, even if God directs it, will not atone for your sins. Only one Man can do that. Remember, we are born with a sin nature, and even if we strive to do good things, we cannot earn our way into heaven or into convincing God to love us any more than He does.

One of my spiritual mentors made this analogy that has stuck with me: If I were cooking an omelet for you for breakfast, and I cracked two good eggs into the pan but the third was rotten enough to make a dog gag, I could try to rationalize that two good eggs should outweigh the one bad one. But you would unlikely be able to eat that omelet. Good works, volunteering, charity work, self-sacrifice, or running across a country can't undo the bad things we've done. If we approach accomplishing great things for God as some sort of method of atonement, we will be forever pursuing a higher goal to assuage our feelings of guilt—feelings that only an understanding that we are unconditionally loved can truly heal.

My problems were unique to the human experience. Mountains aren't human, and they can't relate to my experience in the slightest. For help, I didn't need a *what*, I needed a *who*.

BETTER THAN MOUNTAINS

During a weeklong camp the summer of my sophomore year, I encountered something new in the kids I was with—it was that *who* I had desperately wanted. I thought my fellow campers were holding out on me, but whatever it was they had, I wanted it too. They introduced me to Jesus of Nazareth, and I instantly knew *He* was the answer I had previously been looking to the mountains to provide. From that moment on, the mountains became a signpost pointing to the Creator *of* the mountains.

Have you ever had a spiritual experience in the mountains? Like on a deep powder day or sitting beside a peaceful lake or standing on the summit of a peak? You know that energy? Well, it's not the mountain; it's not the universe. It's creation's neon sign pointing to the God of the Bible and His Son Jesus.

On that warm summer evening, I invited Jesus to be the leader of my life, but in reality, His leadership in my life took many steps to develop.

God knew me so well, and He knew just how to get my attention. I was a rowdy and rambunctious kid, but I wasn't necessarily naughty or mean or wicked. God knew exactly how to pull me in and save me. What I didn't have was anyone to disciple me. Discipleship is the process by which someone shows us how to live out the life change that starts when we choose Jesus.

Unfortunately, it didn't take long for my "whole new world" to crash land back on the old one. The moment faded; the life change didn't bloom and flourish but instead wilted. Without someone to mentor or disciple me, I went right back to the way I had been living.

CHAPTER 4

PLANS FOR THE FUTURE

If we feel a desire for something that no experience in this world can satisfy, the most probable explanation is that we were made for another world.

– C.S. Lewis

I had grand plans for my future—be a climber and ski bum. My friend Ben and I spent our time climbing around on the mountains. We had already climbed Mount Rainier once and had our eyes set on climbing Mt. Hood after we graduated from high school. That was the sum total of my plan for the future.

My mom had a different plan; she wanted me to betray everything I held sacred and get a *job*. I was packing my gear and getting ready for my climbing trip to the West Coast when she gave me an ultimatum:

"If you pack up to go climb Mount Hood, you might as well pack up all your stuff and not come back. If you go on this climbing trip, you won't have a house to come back to."

I remember thinking that she had just made moving out really easy on me. In any healthy parent/child relationship, eventually the parent and the child must experience a break so that the relationship can reform as a different kind, but I did not have a healthy progression. It was a displaced fracture! Because of the way I was living—rebellious and wild, despite my experience at camp—I had pushed away from my mom, who had been hovering over and smothering me and who had never remarried because I was her life. She was trying to do what was best for me, and it was probably very traumatic when I called her bluff and moved out.

I had a crush on this cute girl and followed her to the youth group trying to get close to her, but I ended up getting closer to God instead (which is better). I moved my stuff into the basement of the youth pastor's house, and he took me in and loved on me, which I now know I needed desperately. At the end of the summer, I moved away to Aspen where I got a job as a lift operator—my dream come true! I was a real Colorado ski bum, living the iconic ski-bum life I had dreamed of. But at the end of the season, I took a job with Chuck Miles, my youth pastor, another of the mentors from my life who have meant so much to me.

Chuck's friend Pat Prag invited me to come live at his place. It was only a mile from the job site where I would be working under Chuck, a general contractor. I was learning carpentry, and Pat was a mountain guide and rock climber—this looked perfect!

I moved all my stuff into Pat's basement, and the very first night I was at the house, he said, "Brian, I want you to get all your climbing gear and show it to me." I thought that we were about to have some fun talking about gear, and I loved gear! "Is that it?" he asked. I had my ski gear still packed up, so he told me to go get it too. A few trips later, all of my outdoor gear was strewn across the basement floor. I was imagining all the trips and adventures we would go on while I lived with Pat and his family.

Instead, Pat said, "Okay, I want you to put all that stuff in the closet, and I don't want you to touch it or look at it or think about it for as long as you live here."

Say what? That was not what I was expecting.

I had never lived with a man in charge of his house, and all I could think was, *Who do you think you are, anyway?* I was torn between thinking that he couldn't tell me what to do and just being shocked . . . and shocked won! I did it. I stuffed all my stuff, my precious gear, in the closet. At that moment, he didn't even tell me why.

One of the many things that Pat helped me see was that I was looking to the mountains and adventure to fill the empty place in my heart—a hole that no amount of adventure or gear could ever fill. Those things, though they were not bad, did not have the capacity to fill that emptiness inside me. People talk about being born again; my time with Pat was like my gestation. I came out of the womb—also known as Pat's basement—having pursued a deeper relationship with the Lord.

In those nine months, I also discovered that my whole identity was wrapped up in climbing and skiing and everything else I did in the mountains. Pat completely deconstructed my identity and showed me how empty I really was. He knew that these pursuits and interests had to be uprooted before God could plant what He wanted in my life. Let me tell you, those things had deep roots that went down to the very core of my being. If I had allowed those roots of a false identity taken from my outdoor activities to grow, I would have easily turned God's next step for my life into a full-on obsession.

Many people don't ever think about this, but blessings in our lives—like the mountains in mine—can become curses if we don't handle them rightly. They can actually become toxic to our lives. When the people of Israel left captivity in Egypt, the Egyptians gave them gold and jewelry and many gifts, but they used that gold to make idols for themselves in the desert while Moses was up on a mountain getting the Ten Commandments. Something God had meant for a blessing turned into an idol, and this can happen with gifts in our lives as well.

God had to purify His people, and that's what He did with me through Pat's leadership. God had wired me for a sense of exploration, adventure, and pushing boundaries, but if I looked to these things for my sense of identity, they would have become toxic. With the root pulled up, God was getting me ready to use those very things I'd laid down again, but in the right way this time—as the blessings He had intended them to be.

DO MORE THAN YOU THINK YOU CAN

Pat and Chuck were both men among men, Marlboro Men I'd have called them back when that was acceptable to say. From them, I learned hard work and toughness. From Pat, I learned that the most important thing in life you can ever do is follow God with all your heart. He modeled it with the way he lived every day, and he defined himself as a man who lived his life in obedience to the leadership of Jesus. I had grown up with my mother and grandmother, an only child with no man around, so living with Pat was a whole new experience. I remember sitting around the dinner table with his family and watching Pat demonstrate what it looks like to be a man, a husband, a father, a leader. I had a fear of Pat that continues to this day — he is a man of few words who oozes confidence and authority.

And I, of course, worked for Chuck Miles, who was even tougher than Pat, not to mention a part-time youth pastor. Chuck had this sweet 1976 Ford F150 with six inches of lift and big thirty-five inch tires. It was loud! But Chuck was also tender; when filling up that beast, it wasn't uncommon for him to bless someone by buying their tank of gas. He never had any money because he was always giving away what he did have. That's what he did for me—he poured out of himself to teach me about working hard.

I didn't like hard work; I liked having fun. Chuck corrected that. I can remember one time he picked me up from Pat's house early on a Saturday morning and drove me to a job site. He told me we needed to clear all the rocks off the lot. (There's a reason they call them the Rocky Mountains—these things were everywhere.) He gave me a wheelbarrow, gloves, and a shovel, and he told me to dig them up and pile them off to the side. Then he took off in his big, loud truck, leaving me and one other guy there the entire day by ourselves. He popped in at noon with Kentucky Fried Chicken® for lunch, hung out with us for a while, and then told us to get back after it—he'd be right back.

"Right back" turned out to be at dusk. "I've got a surprise for you guys," he told us. I thought it would be a check and some dinner, but instead it was these big work lights! "Here, let me set these up for you," he offered before shouting, "Okay, keep up the good work!" And then he drove off again.

He left us there long into the night. It turned into a fourteen-hour workday, but the thing was, no one complained to Chuck. He worked harder than anyone, so no one complained to him. He modeled for me the value of hard work and sticking with something, in addition to teaching me a trade. From Chuck Miles, I learned sometimes you've just got to put your head down and get 'er done.

I always thought I would impress Chuck when I finished a project because he had inspired me to do more than I thought I could. But he always just acted like he had known I could do it the whole time. He saw something in me that I couldn't see in myself.

I sometimes think that Chuck and Pat were running along with me in Mongolia. They both drew something out of me. They saw a glimmering potential to be more and do more than I thought I could do. They challenged me to get 'er done, to push through.

You may not yet have had this opportunity—working with a mentor who saw something in you and drew it out. But let me be the one that speaks a truth to you that will change your life: you're capable of doing more than you think you can. No matter what you're doing, who you are, what's against you, or how hard it is; you can do more than you think you can. You have to push on, push through—strong to the finish.

NO COMPARISON

Pat introduced me to his friend Lynn Sanson who lived in Estes Park, Colorado. Lynn was running an education center at the YMCA of the Rockies. Soon I found myself in a job filled with outdoor adventure again. So it was like I got handed off from Pat and Chuck to Lynn Sanson who became another mentor to me. I worked for him and lived in Estes Park for five years, and during the summer he began a rock climbing and guiding program. All the passions I had walked away from as an identity I now had the opportunity to bring back into my life but in their proper place.

Lynn was about ten years older than me, and he had a wife and two kids. We worked together every day, and we spent a lot of time together, even on weekends climbing in Rocky Mountain National

Park. Among other things, Lynn mentored me in the art of alpine climbing. There are lots of different types of climbing, and I really enjoyed this kind—climbing high up on remote mountain peaks, complete with ropes and protection gear.

One day, Lynn and I snuck out of the office and headed out rock climbing, which you didn't need to twist my arm to do. We drove to a local caging area called Lumpy Ridge, and we set out to do some trad climbing (a form of high-angle rock climbing where protective gear is placed to prevent a fatal fall) on a route called Melvin's Wheel. We scampered down the trail, giggling like a couple of schoolgirls playing hooky. Melvin's Wheel is about three or four pitches—a pitch is a rope length, typically fifty meters—of 5.8 climbing, and it was a beautiful bluebird day in May. Everything in the world was perfect.

At the top of the second pitch, there's a magnificent belay ledge just big enough to sit on and dangle your legs off. We were hundreds of feet off the ground, harnessed in but in a sense dangling off the cliff face. From there, you can feast your eyes on a commanding view of the entire Estes valley and the foreboding peaks of Rocky Mountain National Park beyond. Sitting on that ledge, I remember thinking that life couldn't get any better than this.

Then Lynn said something that shocked me because it felt like he was reading my mind. "You know, Brian, this has been a great day of climbing, but not even this day can come close to even the worst day with my family. I would gladly trade the best day of rock climbing for any day of spending time with my family."

It blew my mind—I literally thought this was as good as life could get. But Lynn, a man I look up to and admire, and who shares my love of climbing and adventure, was telling me it was nothing compared to how much he loved his family. At the time, I remember thinking that he must be crazy—dehydrated! But he wasn't, and I could tell by his life it was true. He lived that daily.

From Pat, I learned what a man is like. From Chuck, I learned hard work. But Lynn taught me how to cherish and put family first. Believe it or not, this love of my family, the formative influence of watching men like Pat and Lynn, is what helped me make the decision to bring our children with us to Mongolia.

THE GIRL FROM MINNESOTA

During the winters, a gang of us climbing bums would migrate over to Winter Park, Colorado, to ski until the snow melted. Then we would scurry back to Estes Park. One winter I met a girl from Minnesota— Lissa. She had just graduated from college and was doing the ski-bum thing, too. We hit it off right away and became best friends. We spent two winters in Winter Park falling in love.

One fall, Lissa and I decided to try out a new ski town for the season. We flipped a coin to decide between Telluride, Colorado, and Jackson Hole, Wyoming. Jackson won. Shortly after heading to Jackson, we found ourselves attending an awesome church in a log building pastored by a bushy-haired man named Mike Atkins.

We were married in June of 1999 in Jackson Hole. Pastor Mike did the wedding, and he co-officiated it with Chuck Miles, who came up for the wedding. Lynn Sanson made it, but Pat Prag couldn't because he was busy surfing in Hawaii (I forgave him).

I became involved in youth ministry there at Jackson Hole Christian Center, which is now called River Crossing. I even became the youth pastor, and I worked as a ski instructor.

And something interesting happened: I fell in love with encouraging young people. And suddenly I was so glad that God had taken the root of climbing and skiing out of my heart because were that still there, I don't know that I would've fallen in love with youth ministry the way I did. I felt like I had found my real purpose in life, my sweet spot.

No matter how much I loved the mountains and climbing and skiing and adventure, when I stepped into youth ministry and mentoring people, I realized that I was born for it. Adventure in the great outdoors took a backseat to pursuing a new passion of encouraging and loving people.

CHAPTER 5

PUTTING OUR YES ON THE TABLE

Only those who risk going too far can possibly find out how far one can go.

– T.S. Eliot

Our life in Jackson Hole, Wyoming, was amazing. We built two houses while we lived there—a little log house that we sold to buy a piece of property on which we built the second. I used the skills I had learned from Chuck Miles, and with the help of my father-in-law, we built two beautiful homes.

However, God was not done getting us ready yet. Helping people was definitely a calling, and I naturally excelled at it. But raw, undeveloped talent can only get you so far. In 2007, I felt a pull to go back to school. I hadn't been to college yet (remember, my plan had been to graduate from high school and excel at being a ski bum), and I wasn't sure where I should go.

Lissa and I searched the country for a school that matched what was in our hearts, and Oral Roberts University popped up on our radar. When we read the mission statement, we realized it lined up with our core values and a mission statement we had for our family. Founder Oral Roberts felt God had called him to "Raise up your students to hear my voice, to go where my light is dim, where my voice is heard small, and my healing powers not known, even to the uttermost bounds of the earth. Their work will exceed yours, and in this I am well pleased."

I enrolled as a thirty-four-year-old freshman at ORU in the very not mountainous home of all things not alpine, Tulsa, Oklahoma. I joined the staff of a great local church as a part-time youth pastor of fifth graders, and I eventually graduated from ORU after three years with a theology degree. I later came on as a full-time elementary children's pastor at our church.

50K

During my years in Tulsa, I really missed the mountains. I had spent most of my life in them, so there was really no way to scratch my itch for adventure in the small foothills of the Ozark Mountains. Tulsa has few rocks to climb, no mountains, nowhere to ski, and limited mountain biking. And road biking in Tulsa is just dangerous! All of which led me to casually picking up running. I had no ambition or goals for my running, but I needed some exercise and a way to get outside. I had never done much running, so I thought it would be a good new challenge.

A friend of mine from ORU, Jeff, suggested that we do a fifty-kilometer trail race, which works out to about thirty-two miles. I thought it sounded like fun, so we started training for the race. What we didn't take into account was that the race was only about ten weeks away! We needed to fast-track our training. We went from basically not doing any running to doing more than a marathon in nine weeks.

There is a terrific scene in Star Wars® (no, not the new ones, the real Star Wars®) where Han Solo says, "Never tell me the odds!" I have no idea how many times I have done something "impossible" simply because I didn't know any better. I didn't know it couldn't be done, so I accidentally did it.

Running the trail race was like that; nobody told us that we couldn't or shouldn't train for a race like that in less than ten weeks. So we did!

And you know what? We did it! We both finished the race. Now, I hobbled like a ninety-year-old invalid for two weeks afterward, but I finished the stinking race. At the time, I thought, "Well, that was fun. I'll never do that again!"

Little did I know . . .

MONGOLIA FOUND ME

It was about a year after that temporarily crippling run when I first watched a documentary called The Long Way Around about two guys riding their motorcycles all the way around the world. I loved the adventure of it. As they rode across Mongolia, I was absolutely captivated by the countryside—the ruggedness of the terrain and sheer scope of it. We call Montana "Big Sky Country," but let me just tell you: because of its flat expanses, Mongolia has it beat! Then there are the Mongolian people—appearing to be frozen in time, a lost people a century out of date.

The explorer in me was instantly drawn to the country of Mongolia, and as I watched these two guys ride, drag, sweat, and cuss their way across the country, a little ridiculous thought popped into my head.

It would be really cool to do a trail run in Mongolia.

Right on the heels of that thought was that if I were going to do a small trail run in Mongolia, I might as well run across the entire country.

I remember looking around the room like, "Who said that?"

A couple weeks went by, and I didn't do anything more with that thought. After all, it was insane. I told my friend Jeff about it, but then I forgot all about Mongolia because of family, work, and life. A year slowly passed, and during that time, the thought of running across Mongolia would occasionally bubble up. I'd think about it, chewing on the idea like a cow with its cud. I'd roll it around in my head before dismissing it as an unrealistic, selfish, Peter Pan fantasy.

But then it would bubble up again. I had idea reflux that just wouldn't go away.

After about a year of this bubbling-up-and-pushing-it-back-down cycle, I began to think that perhaps this wasn't just Brian having a midlife crisis. (I was almost forty years old, so it wasn't out of the question). But after regurgitating this idea numerous times, it began to occur to me it might actually be God. And then I finally had the novel thought of praying about it.

"Lord, is this of You? Do You want me to run across Mongolia?"

If it were, I wanted to know why and how—two of several very silly questions we tend to ask God.

When we ask why or how, I almost think God chuckles. God does not owe us any of those answers; He never promises to answer those types of questions in the Bible. Any time we get an answer from the Lord on a why or how question, it is purely His graciousness to answer. Now, don't misunderstand—God is not amused by making us uncomfortable by withholding answers. Most times those issues are simply not our job to worry about.

PARADISE WITHOUT PURPOSE IS PRISON

We had the chance to go back to Jackson Hole to visit friends and have a little vacation in the summer of 2011. By this point, I was praying about Mongolia and seeking God's direction for us as a family, so we spent a lot of time praying about it while we were in Wyoming. But the only thing I felt like I really came away with was this: "Paradise without purpose is prison."

If that sounds cryptic enough to be on a fortune cookie to you, too, then you understand how confused I was. I thought, Okay, that's great, but what does it mean?

This is not the first time I've felt like I got this kind of response. I have learned that when God does not explain something further, He is saying, "You go figure it out." Proverbs tells us that it's God's privilege to conceal things, but it is our privilege to discover them.[3] Remember, God does not owe you answers to why and how questions.

But there's an important distinction to make here: God does not hide things from us; He hides things for us—to find like buried treasure.

As I prayed and read the Bible, chewing on this statement that "Paradise without purpose is prison," here's what I uncovered.

We thought something like going back to Jackson Hole would have been paradise for us. People had offered us jobs, a place to live, and more. We could easily have moved back "home."

But right then, it would not have been part of the bigger plan for our lives.

We could move back to our "paradise," but it would be like a prison to us because it wasn't part of the plan for that stage of our lives. We would have missed God's purpose for us right then, in that moment.

So we had to lay down our own ideas and plans in exchange for what we thought God's were—His purpose and His timing. We had to

---

3   Proverbs 25:2

decide that wholeheartedly buying into His plan was our new paradise, no matter where that was or what we were doing. We had to surrender our own view of "paradise" not unlike I'd had to let the climbing go years before.

It was shortly after that I started to understand what we were supposed to do in Mongolia. It's funny that somewhere halfway across the world, with vast stretches of open sky to rival Montana yet no scenic culture could be considered "paradise" for us. But because God wanted us there, we were going to discover exactly how empowering being fully in His will can be.

Paradise without purpose is indeed prison, but being in God's will and purpose for your life can transform your prison into a paradise. Make sure that you're seeking God's will for your life, so when He drops something in front of you, big or small, you're ready— ready to say "yes," no matter what it is. Because if you ask, "Well, what about _____?" and get hung up on the details instead of moving to obey, you could be waiting for answers for quite a while.

FAITH COMES IN INCHES

Life certainly confronts us with a lot of "what ifs." Following what you feel God would like to do in your life, interestingly, is often no different. We had a huge number of "what ifs" about Mongolia, and any one of which (and certainly any combination of them) could have kept us from proceeding. So many details hung in the balance. What if this weren't actually a God thing and were some kind of midlife crisis? What if we couldn't raise the money? What if I couldn't keep my job? What if one of us got hurt or sick? What if I couldn't really run the miles every day?

There's a word for letting God "sweat" those details—faith. People will sometimes throw out the phrase "faith walk" to describe what it's like trying to follow and obey the will of God. They may use grand theological terms to describe it, but to me it mostly looks a lot like a scene from an old Indiana Jones® movie:

Confronted with a seemingly impossible obstacle, a giant chasm, Indy has only some notes jotted in a book to give him assurance that somehow, some way, crossing the gap is possible. "You must believe," his father, played by Sean Connery, whispers from where he lies. The older Jones has been shot, and unless Indy solves the problem, his father will die.

In tackling this challenge, Indy seems sure to fall to his death. But if he doesn't act, his father will certainly die. After calming himself, eyes closed and hand over his heart, Indy raises one foot over the impossible gap, and he steps out, seemingly into nothingness, only to find that his foot touches something solid—a narrow stone path that he could not see.

It was not the cliché leap of faith—it was one step into the void.

"Big steps" in our walk of faith are often like this—we have to seek peace in our hearts, cling to what we know of God's character, and (often awkwardly) step out. God will typically not tell us why or how; He simply asks us to come out to Him, walking on the water as Peter did coming to Jesus.

A lot of people look at what we did in going to Mongolia and think that we happily charged off in blind faith, and because it worked out they say, "Oh, well, you were lucky." They didn't know how many "what ifs" and other questions were staring us down and challenging us like a horde of deadly orcs closing in around Frodo and the others in the Fellowship of the Ring. However, God has provided a secret weapon. It isn't a silver bullet to magically slay all your problems, but it will make all the difference when you are facing down an angry horde of "what ifs."

God didn't answer my why and how questions for me. He let me wrestle with the idea . . . for two years.

During this time, I had several casual conversations with my wife about this crazy idea. She often used the tried-and-true tactics of dismissing it or changing the subject when I would bring it up. She knew me well by now: I'm notorious for biting off more than I can chew when it comes to adventures. She also knew me well enough to know if I was talking about it, I was going to try to find a way to make it happen . . . at least, eventually.

She may have thought I was crazy, but she definitely thought that while it was a noble ambition and great adventure, it simply wasn't possible. I thought the same thing, honestly.

Turns out we were both wrong. The only right one was God.

FORGOTTEN CHILDREN

So I began to do research. First of all, where in the world was Mongolia? I found it. Second, how far across lengthwise is it? I learned that too. Third, had anyone ever run across it before? Not that I could find.

As I read about the country of Mongolia, I soon discovered a group of people that the world, seemingly, even Mongolians, had forgotten about. These people were not isolated herdsman or migrants; they were the children of the capital city of Mongolia, Ulaanbaatar.

It turns out that until about twenty years ago, Mongolia had been under the Soviet labor movement and heavily indoctrinated with communism. Russia had funded the country, and it was basically a communist state. When the USSR crumbled, Russia pulled out of Mongolia and left the country in a tailspin financially, politically, and culturally. A one-two punch then hit Mongolia: one of the worst winters in recent history joined this political upheaval. This catastrophic cold spell killed off a great deal of livestock, further damaging an agrarian economy.

In a country of under 3 million people, nearly half of them now live in the capital Ulaanbaatar, but that number wasn't always so high. The rest of the country's relatively young population is made up of nomadic herdsmen living out in the countryside. The devastating freeze killed off many of their animals, and the nomadic families, having lost their livelihood, flooded into the capital city looking for food and work and help of any kind.

What they found was that life in Ulaanbaatar is very difficult because tens of thousands of other people, basically refugees in their own country, strained a system that hadn't worked for the Soviets and certainly didn't work without their backing. Families were shattered, and starving parents just trying to find enough to eat abandoned their children.

Passion grew in my heart as I read about the epidemic of homeless children living in the streets of Ulaanbaatar, the coldest capital city in the world. Few, if any, state-run resources are available to these children—no orphanages or welfare programs to take them in. In the Christian world, historically churches have stepped up to take care of what government cannot (which should be the other way around), but this is not the "Christian" West. This is Mongolia, a virtual desert for Christianity after roughly seven decades of religion-destroying communism. There is no established "church presence" in Mongolia. And as a result, without state help, literally thousands of children are homeless on the streets of the capital city of Ulaanbaatar.

The entire country of Mongolia hovers around four to five thousand feet above sea level; Ulaanbaatar sits at 4,430 feet. Because of its relatively high elevation, latitude, and weather conditions, Ulaanbaatar is the world's coldest capital city—one resource calls it nearly a subarctic climate. Winter nighttime temperatures can average well-below zero degrees Fahrenheit, and homeless children are out in it day after day, season after season.

The orphans used to be underground. Beneath the city streets, they escaped the cold by retreating into the steam tunnels where Cold War-era plants pumped superheated water through underground pipes to massive Soviet apartment cities. The children could escape the brutal cold by literally steaming in stifling conditions that could be close to 100 degrees. Imagine the brutal extremes during the winter: biting cold above ground or scorching heat underground.

But now even this steaming resource is cut off. After years of the children hiding in the sewer systems, the government welded shut the manhole covers all over Ulaanbaatar, cutting the children off from this brutally hot shelter.

Like the trash of their painfully evolving culture, the children of Ulaanbaatar now live at the city dumps. Discarded like so much garbage, forgotten by families and government alike, these children cling to a meager and terrible survival.

It hit me as I read of their plight that I must help these children. I needed to do something—anything. As a children's pastor with a passion for young people, my heart broke for them. I wanted to do anything that I possibly could to help them.

But what could that be? I didn't have resources to donate or friends in high places from whom to raise funds. I was just one man. What could one person do in the face of so much need?

THE POWER OF AGREEMENT

Influenced by my new burden for the children of Ulaanbaatar, I began discussing the situation in more earnest with Lissa. She and I went around and around for a few weeks, talking about whether or not it was God prompting us to do something for these children—and how. It was actually a big source of tension.

It was now the end of summer 2012, and I had been thinking and praying about Mongolia for about two years. Our "talks" weren't getting us anywhere. I desperately wanted to do something, but I wasn't going to do anything without the complete support of my wife. I also knew that I couldn't talk her into it with my wit and charm because as soon as she talked to other sane people, they were sure to talk her out of it.

But my sense of urgency was growing, and I well remember the day things came to a head. Lissa and I were sitting at Camille's Sidewalk Café. The people around us probably thought we were in the middle of some horrible domestic difficulty because, like an ogre, I was pounding the table and Lissa was in tears and yelling at me.

I hadn't thought about it this way, but my two-year journey of regurgitating my thoughts on Mongolia had led me to a decision: God wanted me to go, so I had already put my yes on the table. However, married people are no longer individuals: they are two who have become one. I was not going to move forward without my better half, but I wanted her to want this too. I wanted her to read the decision for herself that this was motivated by God.

The funny thing was she already had.

Lissa was wrestling with all of this because she was having a great deal of difficulty with the how and why. She is very detail oriented; I am a big picture dreamer. I like to leap and then look; she likes to do the math, compute the drag coefficient, and get the trajectory before she jumps. This is an awesome combination when we use one another's strengths, but there at the restaurant, it only served to butt our heads together.

Through tears of frustration and anger, which were directed toward me, Lissa abruptly said, "Okay, okay, okay. We'll go to Mongolia."

Wait, what?

"I don't want to talk you into this," I said.

Head down, Lissa shook her head as she said, "No, I need to tell you about something. Seven years ago, God actually told me this moment was going to happen."

I hadn't known that. I was all ears now.

Seven years before, while we were on staff at the little church in Jackson Hole, Wyoming, a member of the church went to Mongolia on a missions trip to work with the nomadic herdsman. As he was a horse trainer, he used this as a way of connecting with the people of Mongolia. When he returned, he gave a presentation on the country, and God whispered to Lissa's heart.

"He told me that someday you will go to Mongolia," she told me. "I just didn't think it would be like this!"

She still did not like the idea, but something was changing in her heart. Despite her questions and misgivings, my amazing wife had just decided to put her yes on the table in obedience, not to me but to God. She was willing to take that faith leap right next to me.

In that moment, we came into agreement, which is a powerful thing when any two people do it. But it is absolutely incredible when a married couple does it together with the Lord. Two months of wrestling had finally culminated, not in me winning, but in God winning. Lissa submitted not just to my leadership and the vision that God has given me but to the vision He had given her years before I even knew where Mongolia was. What is really cool is that when Lissa put her yes on the table, instead of succumbing to my arguments with the caveat that responsibility was solely on my shoulders for our fate, her obedience put the plans on the Lord's shoulders. We gave Him lordship over and responsibility for the success or failure of our venture. We were fully committed and in unity with Him and each other.

Together.

The key to facing down the army of "what ifs" that can attack the vision God has given you is obedience—it's saying yes to Him even before you have all the answers. You do not turn a blind eye to reality or wear denial like some rose-colored glasses—"what ifs" are often legitimate. But when you've already decided to obey and you are committed to saying yes to God, it puts all those questions into perspective that God is faithful to work out the details even before you have all the answers.

So when God calls you to obey Him on something big or small, your secret weapon is deciding to obey Him no matter what. Take down your "what ifs" one at a time, and just keep saying yes to God.

CHAPTER 6

AGREEMENT THROUGH TEARS

Security is mostly a superstition. It does not exist in nature, nor do the children of men as a whole experience it. Avoiding danger is no safer in the long run than outright exposure. Life is either during adventure, or nothing.
– Helen Keller

Lissa had long ago learned that she took care of the details, and I was the guy with the big ideas. When I first told her about running across Mongolia, we were on vacation back in Jackson Hole. Long before our conversation at Camille's Sidewalk Café, I had dropped the bomb on her that I felt God was drawing me to run across a country.

When I told her, "I feel that God is calling me to run across Mongolia," she actually knew then from years of experience dealing with me that it was going to happen, she told me later. She just didn't know what form it would take. Lissa knew that I wasn't in the habit of just throwing out wild, harebrained ideas; I was in the habit of *doing* them!

At that point I only had two concrete details to bring to my detail-oriented wife: we were going to run across Mongolia—the width of the country—and that it was to be in the summer of 2013. That was it.

I had let the pot simmer with Lissa for a few months, stirring it every thirty days or so before the yes-moment over lunch. Part of the problem had been that I would bring it up at inconvenient times, like when Lissa's attention was divided between me and the kids or one of the other many dynamics that drive daily life. Our decisive lunch meeting was our attempt to set a time and place to tackle the big discussion—a technique I highly recommend for married couples. Big discussions need intentional planning.

Lissa wanted details. How long would it take? Would we have to quit our jobs? How would we raise the financial support to cover expenses? What would the kids do? How would we work out the logistics?

When she had seen the horse trainer's presentation on Mongolia and felt God tell her we would go one day, Lissa had thought that it looked like a cool, crazy place to camp. But there was no timetable, no pressure. God's call seven years ago was indistinct. Now we had a goal and a timetable:

Across Mongolia. Summer 2013. Details to be announced.

Unity is a very powerful thing. When Lissa had decided to put her yes on the table, she asked, "What do you need from me?"

"We need to both agree this is happening." I knew that if we could both agree that this was God's will for our family and that we would obey, we could work out the details.

It's easy to give in to the temptation to put the details first and then think we will commit after we have them. The problem is God rarely operates this way. Throughout the Bible, we have examples of God calling and then His people responding with very little concrete information. Abraham received God's call to leave the country of his father and go to a land that God would show him. God didn't say where to stop, only to go—and that He would tell Abraham when to stop going. Peter didn't get a water-walking tutorial before he stepped out of the boat; he simply put his foot out over heaving waters and stepped toward Jesus.

If you're looking for details, there often are times you are going to be disappointed. Depending on your personality type, this may be more difficult for you than for others. As a leap-first kind of guy, I probably had an easier time jumping into commitment and then asking questions later than my wife, but this is one of the things that makes us such a great team.

With our agreement in place, our yes opened the door for Lissa's gift of details and organization to kick in, and the moment we both said yes, a total peace settled over us. Where before there had been tension and unrest and struggle, our fights about Mongolia turned into battle planning.

It's easy to put the cart before the horse—to get the invitation from God and start trying to answer all the "what ifs" before saying yes. God is not obligated to give us answers to our *how* or *why* questions; He's looking for our *yes* or *no*. We want answers before we commit, but what I've found is that when I put my yes first, it puts my "what ifs" into perspective. That perspective looks like a confident assurance that though I don't know how, it is going to work out.

SIGN ON THE DOTTED LINE

If you have signed a service agreement or contract lately, you're probably aware that there is an awful lot of fine print these days. If you've ever bought a house, it's not just pages of documents—it feels like a book's worth! You sign your name so many times, you have a cramp at the end of the day.

However much legalese you have to wade through, any and all contracts and agreements are signed at the end, only after you have (supposedly) read everything thoroughly. The crazy thing is God doesn't work the same way we do down here. In fact, God turns the whole thing on its head. He wants your signature before you read the fine print.

When God first dropped the dream of running across Mongolia in my heart, I felt like I was sitting across the table from Him, and He slid a thick stack of documents across the table to me. On the cover page were the simple terms of the contract: "Across Mongolia in 2013, and raise awareness and support for orphans in the capital city." Below that was a place for two signatures, one for Him (already signed) and one for me.

Our natural first reaction before signing would be to take off the cover page and read through all the fine print to find out what all is involved in fulfilling the terms of that contract. I desperately wanted to know! But God had no intention of letting me comb through all of those pages, and no matter how many times I asked, I felt like my hand was metaphorically swatted aside and that God said with a wink and a playful grin, "Ah-ah-ah! No peeking. This is the deal—take it or leave it."

When I talk about putting our yes on the table, this is what I mean. It's signing a contract to trust Him and commit before you understand all the terms, conditions, and particulars.

One of the reasons why I feel that God does it like this is because it is a test. It's not a test to show Him what's in our hearts (He already knows). No, it's a test to reveal and expose to us what He already knows is in our hearts. We are masters at self-deception, and it takes a test like this to clear away the lies we tell ourselves and to expose the truth.

Signing before we read the contract reveals to us how much we trust God. We have to trust Him and that He is not tricking us, doing something mean, or giving us a bad deal. Now, sometimes we don't understand the whole picture, and while we carry out the contract, things can seem bad. But the Bible promises that God works all things for our good and that He has a plan for us that will give us hope and a bright future.[4]

God puts the signature page of the contract first because we would typically freak out about what's going to happen in the contract and what He is inviting us to do, but part of God's methodology is to teach us to find our strength in Him. When we accomplish the impossible because we are obeying God, He gets the credit.

You may read all of this and think to yourself that you could never imagine agreeing to your "Mongolia" without reading the contract first. Maybe you feel that you don't know God well enough to trust Him and step out like that. The only thing I can say is that you can't trust someone if you don't really know Him. I encourage you to not write yourself off or to write off your dream too quickly.

When you know His character, you can trust that whatever is in the contract He's asking you to sign without reading is good. He is the only One who is good, and His dreams for you are able to take even the worst things you have experienced and turn them around into a plan for your good.[5]

But before He shows you the details of how He will do that, He requires the trust we call "faith." When you step out in faith, you give

4   Romans 8:28 and Jeremiah 29:11
5   Genesis 50:20

God room to do the impossible. And when you have seen God do the impossible in your life, you'll become something new and different—a dangerous person.

DON'T UNDERESTIMATE THE POWER OF AGREEMENT

A huge help in dealing with the difficulties we encountered was actually the unity. It let us keep one another on track, and there were times we had to submit to one another.

Submission can be a dirty word, even in the church because it has been abused. Lissa described to me that submitting to God and His call on our lives through my leadership on this was actually one of the most freeing experiences she has ever had. Moving from I have to to I get to submit enabled her to step into her gift for details with passion and skill. She got to lay down the burden for the ultimate responsibility, and give it to me while I gave it to God, so then it was all on Him. It was an awesome thing, but like so many other parts of our journey to Mongolia, this transition didn't happen simply with a choice to obey God and go to Mongolia. It started far earlier than that.

When we had our first child, Selah, we had not been married all that long and had planned on leading seventy-five teenagers on an outreach to Peru. We had committed to the trip before we learned that Lissa was pregnant, and at first we didn't think it would be a big deal. However, as the trip approached, so did our due date. In fact, we were closing in on the no-fly date for pregnant ladies. We would slip under the wire by two days.

I kept telling her, "It's okay. You can still go," and encouraged her to go anyway. I didn't think I could do it without her, and the gravity of the situation perhaps had not fully settled on me. Meanwhile, my wife's nesting instincts had already told her that flying to the southern hemisphere nearly eight months pregnant was not a good idea.

She didn't have peace about going, and it actually was a source of great conflict. However, Lissa felt like God told her that if I said she could go, then she would be able to do it. She turned to me in bed one night and said, "If you feel like I'm meant to go with you and you are making that decision for us as a family, then I will submit to your decision and won't mention not going again."

Less than twenty-four hours later, I came to her with something to say, "You're not going."

The moment she put that decision in my hands, to make the choice for her and our little baby, the weight of what I was deciding settled over me. It was sobering. I realized that I couldn't put both of the girls I cared for most in the world in jeopardy just because I didn't want to tackle a youth outreach without the assistance of my soulmate. I looked at the decision differently with the authority as the head of a home. Lissa realized that she had actually been getting in my way of being able to wear that mantle of authority for our family by arguing about it.

So really, she made the switch toward trusting God through me ten years before the decision about Mongolia ever came up. The Peru outreach was probably the first time that this came up, but it certainly wasn't the last. It started a lifestyle of submitting to one another the way God tells us to in the Bible, which enabled us to make the decision about Mongolia and then stick with it.

The Peru outreach experience was definitely on our minds as Lissa and I committed to seeing through whatever God had planned.

THE HARD PART

As improbable as it sounds, the decision to go and the preparation actually seemed harder than the rest of the trip. After everything we did just to get to Mongolia, the running was actually the easy part! You might even say that Lissa and I coming into agreement and putting our yeses on the table may have been the hardest part emotionally.

It was also utterly vital.

If I had talked her into going to Mongolia because "God told me to," when the going got rough, it would put the onus on me. However, just as Lissa came to the Lord on her own, God spoke to her about Mongolia on her own as well. He had to "talk her into it." So the real power was when we put our two decisions to obey God together in unity.

It's important to note that when I first told her about Mongolia, I didn't say, "God is telling us to do this, and you'd better get in line." Instead, I simply told her that I strongly felt God was calling us to go, but I wouldn't go without her. Then I asked her what she felt God was saying to her.

Now, I wasn't making it her decision. That would be unfair of me, but what was vital here was that I submit to her as my marriage partner. Too many macho men are quick to say that wives are to submit to their husbands, but before it says anything about that, the Bible tells us that we are to submit to one another out of reverence for Christ.[6]

Lissa's "wrestling," it turns out, was far more with God than it ever was with me. When she finally put her yes on the table and put her trust in God, not me, it let us come together in unity. We would need that shared commitment to survive the months that were to come.

SUBMISSION 101

Now, over the years we've done this submission thing right . . . and wrong. (By "right" I mean the way God spells it out in the Bible — whether or not it seems culturally relevant. By "wrong" I mean that we also tried to do it religiously or selfishly.) Likewise, we've seen

---

6   Ephesians 5:21-30

other couples do it right and wrong.

Sometimes the wife digs her heels in and fights her husband's leadership; sometimes the husband tries to push, bully, or drag her along. Not doing it God's way (the right way) can easily be either or both spouses' fault.

We learned that oftentimes, a husband really needs to lead better and willingly lay his life down for his wife and his family, preferring their interests above his own. But often she needs to let him be the leader—yes, even in today's egalitarian society.

Lissa broke our stalemate of my pulling and her resisting when she surrendered to God, and I knew in my heart she wasn't trying to use reverse psychology on me. She was not trying to guilt trip me by putting the fate of our family in my hands; she empowered me to take leadership and make Holy Spirit-inspired choices by submitting to my leadership. Really, she was trusting God more than me, and I could sense that. The weight of the mantle of leadership from God fell on me, and it was scary!

And yet again we come back to the fear of the Lord. Lissa empowered me to make the best decision for her and our family, but the fear of the Lord is what put it in proper context.

Have you ever seen a movie preview and realized that you didn't need to see the whole movie—that they'd just shown you all the best parts? Or maybe you've realized the lives that people put up on social media are actually the very best and that they don't show you the worst? Well, this is a little like that. What I don't want you to miss here is that our examples of the Peru outreach and our trip to Mongolia are highlights of our struggle to submit to one another God's way. These two seminal moments stand out as successes, but I won't mention the many failures we've experienced. All, however, built our faith that God could lead and direct our family, we could hear His voice, and that we could operate in our respective roles to carry out His mission.

You have heard the expression, "Practice makes perfect," but perhaps you haven't heard the variation: "Practice makes permanent."

As people trying to do family the way God set it up, we practice in the way a doctor does—daily. Like a doctor, our practice does not result in perfection; it's a way of making something a permanent part of life. Submitting to one another is a way of life for us, and I hope that our noteworthy successes would encourage you to practice this in your own family. I strongly believe that what we accomplished in Mongolia would not have been possible had Lissa and I not practiced submitting to one another, and to God, in our family. God allowed us to perfect our faithfulness in small things so that when the big thing of Mongolia came, we were ready.

NOT READY?

Some of you might be reading this and thinking it sounds all well and good for us—that we'd had lots of practice and were ready—but that you and your spouse haven't rolled like that. All these ideas are great, you might be thinking, if your husband is a man of godly vision or your wife is a woman who will put the responsibility on God's shoulders.

But what about the wife who has a husband with no vision? Or his vision isn't godly? Or what about the husband whose wife thinks submission is a term that goes along with chauvinist pig? Or what about those who are still learning to hear from God or aren't even sure that's truly possible?

When we get to a fork in the road and we aren't practiced in submitting to one another, we typically resort to tactics like manipulation and intimidation. God actually has some specific instructions for husbands and wives to treat each other, but basically it comes down to one simple thing:

We are to put our spouse ahead of ourself. We are to prefer our spouse's needs, weaknesses, and desires over our own and lie ourselves down for them. And if you cannot agree, it's time to put your "Mongolia" on pause—whatever it is.

Some of you may read this and think that sounds nice but that you have to make a big decision now. But let me tell you something—I think the remarkable marriage will let the opportunity go if you're not in harmony on it.

Crazy? Maybe. So are a lot of God's ways—they can seem pretty foolish to us. But that doesn't mean they aren't right; they are. See, I personally believe that God's much more concerned about your spiritual growth and the strength of your marriage growing than He is ever concerned with that new job, new car, or new mobile device.

A great passage in the Bible asks, how "can two walk together, unless they are agreed?"[7] You cannot walk together down the road for the purpose of your life unless you are in agreement.

Agreement is more important than opportunity.

Without the strength of our unity, Lissa and I would never have survived the rigors of Mongolia . . . or even the lead-up before we left, where repeated opportunities and oppositions, which we'll cover shortly, threatened to distract us from our purpose. We were able to stay the course because of our agreement and all the little decisions that had paved the way for agreeing and holding firm on this big one.

Some friends of ours recently told us they were thinking of going to Ghana, Africa, but it quickly became apparent to us that the decisions they were trying to make had outpaced their experience level in hearing from and obeying God. They saw what we did by going to Mongolia and thought it had been easy for us to make that decision.

---

7   Amos 3:3 NKJV

It can indeed seem as though some people are simply born to hear and obey God on some big decision, but the reality is the ability to make a big decision is the result of having been responsible with the smaller decisions. Because of our smaller decisions, we were ready for our Mongolia.

I'd like you to frankly ask yourself: Am I ready for my "Mongolia"? Just stop and dwell on that for a moment. If God has called you to something big right now, have you been faithful in the small things so you can handle a big one? Or do you and your spouse, if you're married, have some groundwork to do?

Okay, if you really paused to ask yourself that question, you have my permission to read on because there's something else you need to know.

ONE GIANT LEAP FOR MANKIND . . . OR THE FIRST BABY STEP?

I want to let you in on one other important secret. You may be thinking that doing something big for God is a giant leap, and perhaps the analogy I gave earlier of Indiana Jones may even reinforce that.

In actuality, doing big things for God is not one giant leap—they're many small steps. Our journey across Mongolia was not a giant leap. How do you run across Mongolia? One step at a time—one step after another after another. Fifteen hundred miles later, people will look at you and say that what you accomplished is a big miracle, but I can promise you it isn't. It took many, many, many ordinary steps.

Do not discount the small things. Don't think that small decisions don't matter, that you can fudge on the little things and then really come through when it's "important." You create your ability to be faithful in the big things by being faithful in the small ones; plus, really big things only seem like that from a distance.

So, if you're not ready, take heart. The proverbial journey of a thousand (or fifteen hundred) miles starts with a single step. Maybe it's time to start taking steps together with your spouse?

Even the biggest things we do for God are the results of many small steps that He leads us on along the way.

The questions are as follows: "Will you follow in His steps?" and "Will you do it in unity with your spouse?"

YOUR VISION

So how do you start building that togetherness, that harmony that will let you walk out those steps together? One of the things that gave us strength to make the choices we did and walk in unity was a vision statement for the whole expedition. Was that our first one? Not at all! (Are you detecting a trend here?)

Before our vision for Mongolia, we had taken the time to write down some of the things God had shown us for our marriage and family over the years. Some of these revelations were so important to us that we sought to make them part of our family DNA.

On our fifth-year wedding anniversary, we treated ourselves to a steak dinner. It wasn't in the budget, but this was our anniversary and we wanted to splurge. As we looked at the past four years, we wondered what the next year held for us. A question suddenly popped into my head: "Why are we married?" As we talked it through, we decided a marriage needs a vision—a mission to accomplish. You wouldn't go into a business venture with no goal or purpose in mind, so should your marriage, family, or life be any different?

It took a while, but we eventually crafted a mission statement for our whole family:

> *From a heart overflowing with love and*
> *gratitude, and using our God-given*
> *gifts and talents, the Hunters exist to*
> *proclaim the good news of the Gospel*
> *and to use our home as an example of*
> *the wonderful life available in Jesus*
> *Christ.*

To help you get started with forming a vision, it can be helpful to think of the top-two things you feel put on this earth to do—the top two things you're best at or love most. Combine your ideas and your spouse's to craft the beginning of a vision statement.

Thoughts like these eventually led to five core values for our family in addition to a vision statement: faith, obedience, family, purpose, and discipline. You may be able to quickly see how the top two, faith and obedience, influenced our decision to say yes to God, but another central one is the concept of family itself. Put really simply, we stick together.

You wouldn't be reading this if purpose weren't important. I think so many people live their lives just to make a living instead of making a difference, but when we live our lives with purpose, we have opportunity to leave a bigger mark on this planet.

The last one is discipline, and the funny thing is that, on my own, I'm probably the least qualified person on earth to talk about it—remember, my goal in life was to be a ski bum! But God has taught me that after the warm fuzzy feelings of being called by God fade in the hot sun, it boils down to just plain old hard work and discipline. Anyone can say they love God, and anyone can take the first step in obedience, but it takes discipline to see it through.

So those are the big ones for us, and they influenced our ability and willingness to follow God's prompting to go to Mongolia. And in carrying out the purpose we felt God was putting on our hearts, we realized quickly that we would step out in faith, obey, and go to Mongolia as a family. And let me tell you, that required some hard work and discipline.

These values gave birth to our mission statement for our trip across Mongolia: "With my family as support, I'm going to run fifteen hundred miles across the entire country of Mongolia to raise awareness and support for orphans and vulnerable children living in the capital city of Ulaanbaatar."

People often ask me about knowing what God's will is for their lives and how to figure out how to make choices. Well, you need a tool for judging things against, and I can't more highly recommend that you sit down and define the core values and mission for you, your family, and the purpose you feel God has given you. When you come to a fork in the road and need to know whether to turn to the right or to the left, knowing the mission God has already assigned to you can make the choice much clearer.

In fact, the only tool better than this is the Bible itself. Your purpose and what God has said work together. God's words to us in the Bible are like the top level of a filter—the big stuff gets filtered out. You don't have to wonder if it's God's will to rob a bank. But then the more intimate understanding of your purpose filters the more personal stuff, such as whether or not a particular job is right for you. If that job requires that you travel forty weeks out of the year but a core value for you is family, you'll know that choice compromises a core value or your vision statement. If it violates a core value, you know it isn't a right choice. If a choice doesn't line up with the Bible, your mission, or your core values, you can filter it out.

On a final note, there are times something will go through your filters and yet seem impossible. Case in point, running across Mongolia. So a final question to ask is, "Can I tackle this on my own?" If the answer is yes, then it may be your own idea rather than a God idea.

See, if it is within your capability and you pull it off, guess who gets the credit? You'll get the pat on the back. And the thing is, God is not in the habit of sharing credit that should go to Him with anyone else. In fact, He specializes in using people who are the least capable and qualified in the eyes of the world. That way, when He pulls it off, it's His name that gets made famous.

So there you have a primer on how we made this decision—using the filter of the Bible, our family vision statement, and our core values. Finally, it met the capability-criteria—it was way out of our league! Only God could pull this off.

The decision made, the plan set in motion, it was time to start telling people. And the first people we told were our kids, who until this point were blissfully ignorant of what we were about to put them through.

CHAPTER 7

OPPORTUNITY AND OPPOSITION

The closer you get to excellence in life, the more friends you'll lose. People love you when you're average because it makes them comfortable. But when you pursue greatness it makes people uncomfortable. Be prepared to lose some people on your journey.
— Tony A. Gaskins, Jr.

It was time to start telling people about Mongolia. So, to break it to our kids, we took them to dinner at Red Robin for awesome hamburgers and milkshakes. We started building it up, telling them that we were going to do something very exciting and adventurous. With a corny drumroll, we announced our plans to raise money for orphans and vulnerable children and to run across Mongolia in the summer of 2013.

"Okay, cool," they said. "Can we have another milkshake?"

I must admit, I had expected more of a response, but oh, to handle life with a child's faith! If only we could all handle big events in our lives with this kind of blissful trust. The next time you receive big news, I challenge you to imagine how a little child would respond. With utter trust in God, I urge you to respond like our kids did: simply enjoy the blessings He's already given you. Don't sweat it, don't blow it out of proportion, and don't stop trusting God.

One other thing, eventually, our daughter Selah realized that being gone for the summer would mean that she wouldn't be able to swim at the local athletic club's outdoor pool. It threatened to be a crisis moment. Gone for the whole summer to Mongolia? What about swimming and all the rest of the fun stuff we normally would do?

We promised we would make it up to her with the adventure of a lifetime. As her parents, we recognized that the opportunity to create memories and have an amazing adventure far outweighed the fun of swimming in a neighborhood pool.

How many times does God have this same type of perspective about events in our lives? How many times do we gripe about missing a summer of swimming when God is trying to give us the adventure of a lifetime?

Too often, I think we want God to give us good but boring blessings in our lives. Yet, if you have read the Bible, you know that followers of God typically did not have experiences that fit this description.

God wants our lives with him to be an adventure, where we must trust Him for each new step. This should be like attending a series of surprise parties, but many of us are too wrapped up in our concerns to enjoy the surprises. We're worried that He's going to drop the ball, that we'll lose the stuff we love, or that what He has in store won't be as good as what we want.

God has the perspective of a parent who knows that the life-changing adventure that He has planned is far better than the plans we had made to swim in the community pool.

So what would happen if we fully trusted God? What would happen if we really thought He was in control, had it figured out, and actually had the best plan?

If we did, I think more of us would succeed in our own versions of crossing Mongolia.

NEHEMIAH AND THE DISTRACTION OF OPPORTUNITY

There is an amazing story in the Bible about a guy named Nehemiah who encounter the same situation. You can read about it in the book of Nehemiah, chapter 6. Around 400 B.C., Nehemiah lead a group of Israelites from captivity in Persia to rebuild the walls of the city of Jerusalem. No sooner than Nehemiah rolled up his sleeves to get to work did he encounter the distraction of opportunity. There were two officials in the region who wanted to "have a meeting" with him about the building project. On one hand, this could have seemed like a great opportunity. If I meet with these guys, they could be a great asset in mobilizing a local work force and adding momentum to the project. But Nehemiah realized that sometimes even good opportunities can be distractions from God's plan for us.

OPPORTUNITY ISN'T ALWAYS WHAT YOU THINK IT IS

The first thing I said, which proved so true, after the historic agreement at Camille's was, "Get ready for opportunity and opposition." In fact, my prediction proved true that very day.

We oftentimes have an attitude that any kind of apparently good opportunity must be from God. It just sort of makes sense in a way. He's got good plans for us to prosper us and not to harm us, right?[8] So

---

8   Jeremiah 29:11

how could a good opportunity in our lives not be from Him? Don't all good gifts come from God?

The thing is, an opportunity can be "not good" for one simple reason: it goes against something else God has told you to do. In the second chapter, I mentioned how important the fear of the Lord is to me. One of the reasons it's so important to cultivate this respect for the Maker of the universe is that, on occasion, you will find that a good opportunity directly conflicts with your marching orders from God.

We had opportunity (and opposition) before the end of *that day*. To start with, I received a job offer, which definitely sounds like a good thing, right? I mean, surely God wants to prosper us and give us a better job instead of making us run across Mongolia, right?

Opposition can be easy to recognize. Ours was. The moment we started telling (a very select few) people about Mongolia, we started getting opposition. Opposition is designed to discourage you, to beat you down. The world uses it like a bludgeon to try to knock you off course or sap your strength to push forward.

Opportunity is a far subtler problem. Opportunities will seek to distract you from the call of God on your life, and because they can so easily disguise themselves as good things, we must get the perspective we need to see things clearly. We must cultivate that healthy fear of the Lord that puts more concern in our souls at the possibility of disappointing Him than in missing out on something "good."

I can't tell you how often opportunity has been the torpedo that took out something God was doing in the life of one of the young people we have mentored. Many times, right after a young person has said that God was urging him to commit to a mentoring relationship, an opportunity disguised as an angel of light appeared. Like a fish lured by a shiny object, we have watched job offers or relationships or other opportunities distract people from what they said God was telling them to do. So we were aware of the possibility this would happen, but the specific distractions that came at us were surprising.

THREE CHOICES

Both Lissa and I were employed at the same church, so after telling the kids but before we told anyone else, we needed to tell our pastors. We went to the number-two pastor at the church and told him that we felt God was calling us to run across Mongolia. His reaction was understandable because it was the same one we had first—that's crazy!

Once he knew we were serious, we got down to details, and he asked what we wanted. We laid it out: we wanted permission to go, we would love it if in some way the church would support it, and we dreamed that we would somehow be able to keep our jobs. After all, we had bills to pay, to say nothing of raising the finances to do any good for the children of Mongolia.

He absorbed all of this and told us that he would talk to the lead pastor about it and get back to us. We had hoped for a more positive answer, but I think both Lissa and I knew in our hearts that God was calling us to a dramatic first step.

During that first meeting and others after, our pastors asked a lot of good questions—the same ones we'd been asking ourselves, actually. But basically, our lead pastor was just trying to determine if we were sure we'd truly heard from God, as any good pastor would. Really, we only had two concrete details God had said: "across Mongolia in the summer of 2013." In the face of all the reasonable, well-thought-out questions the pastor asked us, these two details seemed like pretty thin threads to hang our future on.

We also had lots of meetings with the number-two pastor where we discussed many different scenarios, but in in the end, our church's response was to give us three options. The senior pastor and the associate pastor we'd been talking to sat us down in the senior pastor's office to go over them together.

The first option was to not to go at all, possibly get a raise and a promotion, and feel appreciated. Maybe we hadn't really heard from God, and we could go back to doing children's ministry as though nothing had happened.

The second choice was to go on a short-term trip to Mongolia—a two-week vacation we were due anyway—as a recon trip in the summer of 2014. We could go on the paid two-week trip, get it out of our system, and do the full expedition later.

The third option they gave us was to allow us to go, but we would not have jobs to come back to. Also, I would not be working as long as I'd hoped—my last day would be at the end of January (and we'd planned to go to Mongolia in July). This last detail, especially, was totally unanticipated, and I felt my heart sinking.

This was our worst-case scenario.

They expressed concern for us. They feared that going to Mongolia would break my body, break our finances, and break our marriage. They worried that we would come back broken and then look to them to pick up the pieces.

Just to be clear, our church was not saying that they were against Mongolia; just that the duration and timing were not a fit with the vision for the church. They made it clear that these were our three choices, and there was no negotiating. We were asking for basically the whole summer off, and we knew from being in ministry that everything works on the school year. Churches ramp up in order to hit the school year running, and our trip to Mongolia would interfere with that.

I admit, our first blush reaction was to be upset. How could our church not be more supportive? But later we understood what they were saying and that this trip and our responsibilities with the church were not compatible. While our pastor personally supported us, he understandably could only offer us those three choices. Thank goodness our friendship survived that small bump in the road and our families are still close to this day.

LIONESS

For a moment, I actually was pretty nervous during that sit-down with the two pastors. I'm not trying to be sexist here, but in my experience, my wife and many women have a "security" need that, in some cases, we men may not. They were telling us that any sense of security from my job would be taken away, and I really didn't know how this would hit Lissa. After all, they were raising very legitimate concerns—ones that we'd though of ourselves and were wrestling with.

Our conversation from Camille's immediately came in to play. Because we had already agreed to commit to God's will, the three choices really jumped into sharp contrast. We'd put our yes to God on the table, and anything that wasn't obedience to exactly what He told us simply wouldn't do.

Was not going an option? No. Was going for two weeks an option or going next year? No. The only things we did know were "across Mongolia in the summer of 2013." Because we had already committed to what God was telling us to do, anything that did not line up with that was automatically out.

Then one of the coolest things I've ever seen then happened. With the boldness of a lioness, Lissa said to them, "Let me explain something to you," as she drew this scale on the back of her notebook. "On one side of this are all the negative reasons not to go and all the positive reasons not to go. But on the other end of the scale is one thing, and one thing only—the fear of the Lord. It doesn't matter what gets stacked on this end of the scale, if the fear of the Lord is on the other end, that will win. Every single time. We'll take option three."

I'm not sure I've ever been more attracted to her than I was at that moment. It was decided. We would be obedient to God, no matter the cost.

They were speechless for a moment, very surprised that we would make that choice.

This conversation occurred in the gap between Thanksgiving and Christmas. Soon, I found out my official last day would be February 19, 2012.

Suddenly, the trip became very real. The cost hammered home. Lissa and I had entertained hopes that we would be able to go and then somehow come back to our old jobs. But really I think we both knew, deep down, that obeying God could cost us everything.

The real shocker wasn't necessarily that we would not be able to come back to our jobs; it's how soon the church felt we should part ways. We would have months without income that we had not anticipated. Raising money to go on the trip felt like it would be hard enough; staying alive while we raised that money now seemed even harder.

OPPOSITION

We didn't start telling people about the trip in earnest until around the time I stopped working with the church. Immediately, we began receiving opposition from some of the people we told. At times, it was very discouraging.

Only in retrospect can we now look back at the way things played out and see God's hand at work, even when my job was over, which was so unexpected. I literally had months without work; however, we soon realized there would have been no way that we would have been able to plan for the trip and fundraise while working full time. I didn't know it when we gave our decision to the church, but after the dust settled from our trip and we could process, we could see that God was already orchestrating things the way they needed to happen—whether we understood it or not.

I would not have been able to do a good job both at work and preparing for the trip, and I certainly would not have been able to train if I had been working full time. I wouldn't have done anything well by trying to do it all, so God cut off that which did not need to be in our lives by presenting us with the choice—trust Him and follow, or embrace the opportunity to go down a different path.

Even more, God knew all about some things that He would develop the year after we returned from Mongolia that may never have happened (or would've been compromised) if we had not submitted and obeyed His timing.

It may not seem like it at the time, but God's ways and timing are always the best. It may seem uncomfortable for moment; it may be hard. You may squirm and second-guess and wonder what in the world God is up to. But when you commit your ways to Him, He really does direct your path—and it is the best possible path!

HOW THE SCALE SHOULD TIP

The options our church presented were all reasonable, and we were not offended. To this day, we still have a great relationship with both the church and the pastors. Initially, though, it was a little shocking because we honestly had not thought that I would be done with my job so early.

Lissa still has the drawing on her notebook to this day: a scale with all the stuff we were afraid of on one side and the words the fear of the Lord on the other side. I don't have to tell you that the scale was completely tipped in favor of the fear of the Lord. It was interesting that as we learned of our options, a holy fear of doing anything other than what God had said rose up inside of us. It literally overwhelmed every other concern.

My amazing wife responded to the (well-meaning) opportunity and opposition in our meeting with the church with classic style and made me fall in love with her all over again. Lissa taking the lead in the conversation is something that would never have happened if I had talked her into it. She later told me that her head was screaming how much safer the options our church presented to us were, but her spirit was screaming, "These choices are all compromise!"

The only option the fear of the Lord leaves is total obedience.

NEHEMIAH'S OPPOSITION

Back to the story of Nehemiah. Once the "distraction of opportunity" tactic failed, then came the out-right opposition tactic. The officials, Sanballat and Tobiah the Gershite, (what sinister names!) began an all-out political assault on Nehemiah. They wrote letters back to the king of Persia saying Nehemiah was in rebellion, they spread un-true rumors about Nehemiah trying to control the narrative, and they even tried to physically halt construction. But I love Nehemiah's reaction. Because he had already put his yes on the table to God's plan, he responded to the opposition: "'There is no truth in any part of your story. You are making up the whole thing.' They were just trying to intimidate us, imagining that they could discourage us and stop the work. So I continued the work with even greater determination" (Nehemiah 6:8-9 NLT, emphasis mine).

THE FEAR OF THE LORD VS EVERYTHING ELSE

The only way to deal with opposition is to live and breathe more fear and respect for the Lord than everything else combined. For husbands and wives, another dynamic is the power of agreement that I mentioned earlier—you must be in unity, or circumstances and the enemy will find opportunities to split you apart and undermine God's call on your life.

I had people come up to me and tell me what I was proposing to do was flat-out impossible. After church one Sunday, a guy came up to me and handed me his business card. "I'd like to take you to lunch," he said. I like it when people offer to take me out to lunch! His business card revealed that he was a doctor—an orthopedic surgeon, specifically. We needed a medical professional to accompany us on the trip, so I immediately had thoughts that God was already answering prayers with a divine connection.

Not so much. For about an hour and a half, this doctor gave me all the scientific and medical reasons why what I was proposing to do was medically impossible. He was even more shocked when he found out I wasn't a "runner." He detailed the particular injuries I would inflict on my body, from tendons to ligaments to muscles to joints to bones.

It was a very cogent case against trying to run across Mongolia. Mostly I just chewed my food for the first part of the lunch, but finally I said, "I agree with you completely—it's impossible. But do you know what? It was also impossible for Abraham and Sarah to get pregnant, but they had Isaac. It's impossible for a man to walk on water, but Jesus did it, and so did Peter when Jesus called him out of the boat. If God has not called me to do this, it is completely impossible. I guess we'll just have to see what happens."

He was speechless. That was it for our lunch. He did not volunteer to travel with us as our medical team—unsurprisingly.

Other people got in my face about what I was doing to my family and how irresponsible my actions were, among many other things. Lissa didn't have too many people talk to her about the physical impossibility, but a lot of people asked her how we could do this to our kids. What would happen if one of them got hurt? Many times we were hundreds and hundreds of miles away from the closest hospital— and even a hospital in Mongolia would provide sketchy care at best compared to what were used to in the States.

People brought up legitimate concerns, and we are convinced that their hearts were in the right place. They asked us if we had thought through the consequences. What people didn't realize is that they were actually questioning our ability to hear God, our understanding of His character, our concept of His protection, and our faith in His provision.

Lissa's mom was one of those people who asked us very good— and very hard—questions. However, what was so cool was that she ended up completely supporting us. "If I know anybody who can do this," she told us, "it's you guys." It was a huge testimony to her love and support because she is very much a detail person like her daughter. She had voiced to Lissa the exact concerns Lissa had as a mom, and so when her support was offered, it carried extra weight. Lissa's parents even went the extra mile by paying for Lissa to have laser-eye surgery before the trip so that she wouldn't need contacts or glasses! You might not think that is such a big deal, but there was not a single day that Lissa did not thank God for her loving parents giving her the gift of sight.

We didn't have any outright opposition from our family, but things that many people said could have been discouraging—the enemy wanted to use anything he could to discourage us. We combated any opposition with the strength of our commitment to what God had told us to do. We clung to His words to us and our agreement, but we also did the best we could to use the wisdom gleaned from the comments we received to take practical steps.

One of the biggest sources of contention was that we were bringing our children. A lot of people thought that was crazy. What they didn't know was that we had led an outreach to Egypt and left our children with Lissa's parents for about three weeks years before. They were still very little, but we had the revelation that we would never again do a trip without our kids. (Again, this was a smaller thing that led to us being able to do a bigger one.) It was completely settled in both of our hearts—we wouldn't be apart from our kids.

THE OPPOSITION WITHIN

Many times we can accept and even expect external opposition— we can wrap our heads around that. But often, far more insidious can be the voices within. Before Mongolia, I can distinctly recall three specific things that nipped at my heels like an annoying dog threatening to trip me. The three things I heard were, "You're too old, it's too late, and you're never going to succeed."

These voices dogged my steps no matter what I was doing—from entering the ministry, to going to ORU, to heading to Mongolia. And the killer thing is that they were *inside*. You can shut out or avoid people who are opposing what God has told you to do, but how do you avoid being in your *own head*?

This, my friend, is where you realize you cannot always flee— sometimes you must fight. Put simply, we combated the fear and concerns that the opposition raised with the promises that God had already spoken to us both in His Word and to our hearts personally. We stood on these promises when the hard times came.

I have to admit, as we told people about Mongolia and began to get ready, I felt like we were Frodo shouldering the burden for destroying the Ring of Power. Our shoulders felt very small and Hobbit-like compared to the weight of the task God had assigned us, but we were determined to see it through till the end.

I'm going to give you a spoiler: victory is possible. Whatever massive-seeming thing looms before you, there is light and hope at the end of the tunnel.

I've told you a little about how I feel now that we've returned from Mongolia—*dangerous*. My ability to trust God has skyrocketed.

But let me tell you one other thing: those voices have not been back. They no longer dog my heels because dogs don't mess with dangerous people.

CHAPTER 8

PREPARATION BRINGS PEACE

Daniel-san, never put passion before principle. Even if win, you lose.
– Mr. Miyagi (Karate Kid 2)

Before Lissa and I made our decision together, I felt a great sense of tension; it felt like a wrestling match in my soul. One force was God's quiet whisper urging me to trust Him and submit to His plan; the other force was my mind screaming for self-preservation and rationalization. Lissa, too, was wrestling inside between what God had told her seven years prior and all the practical roadblocks in our way. But once Lissa and I made the decision to surrender to God's plan, our heats both flooded with a supernatural peace.

A number of times so far, I have referred to a sense of peace. Not everyone knows what that feels like, so before we go much further, I want to take just a moment to get into that a little. After all, how will you know when you have an absence of peace if you don't know what the peace itself feels like?

Close your eyes and imagine a beautiful river—gentle moving water lapping at rocks, trees swaying in the breeze. The temperature is just right, there are no bugs, and you're with people you love. Your only concern is sitting your rear end in an inner tube to let the cool water carry you down river while you relax.

God's peace is like the gentle pull of the current of this stream. You can resist the flow any time you want, but when you are in that flow; worry, fear, and doubt feel unnatural—like trying to walk or swim upstream. Going with God's will feels like moving with the most natural, deepest flow of your spirit.

Opportunities that do not resonate with this kind of spirit-level peace are easy to spot when you're familiar with God's peace. Opposition that fights against you stands out. We had all kinds of battles to fight along the way even though we had His peace. We didn't know the details, but we had peace to proceed.

So I have talked about the opportunity and opposition we encountered a lot, but let me take just a few moments to mention some of the peace we experienced—peace in the midst of tests.

A MEASURED RESPONSE

Despite the opposition and the opportunities for distraction that we had to resist, we also witnessed some people responding to us in a very godly way—a way that we want to emulate ourselves. One of those was Pastor Mike from Jackson Hole, who had actually wanted to ask us a life-changing question before we left but listened to an urging from God to hold off.

For all of the people whose opinions we had to discount, his spiritual insight and sensitivity were foundational parts of our lives. Before we committed, we told him what we were thinking and what we felt God had told us to do. If he had said he did not feel that was God, it would have made both of us really question whether or not we had heard correctly.

His immediate response when we told him our plans was that he'd pray about it. That's a great response anytime! We laid it all out before him and asked for his discerning prayers. About a week later, he called us and said that the Lord had pointed him to one verse: "Do whatever he tells you."[9] His counsel to us was solid confirmation that we were on the right track.

It's important to be careful who you trust with the most important, intimate parts of your heart. Plenty of people have an opinion about what you should do, but few have earned the right to speak into your life. Unfortunately, we can sometimes expose important, sensitive parts of our hearts to piggish people we should not.

A friend of mine often says that the only people whose opinions really matter are those who love you unconditionally and sacrificially. Those are the people you listen to most, and Pastor Mike was one of those people in our lives.

Take just a moment to stop and think of who those people are in your life—the people who love you unconditionally and sacrificially. They are the ones who will lift you up in prayer when you tell them about whatever God calls you to do. The right people will pray for you, speak truth to you, and, most importantly, fear and respect God enough to tell you, "Do whatever God has told you to do."

No one can hear from God for you—not ultimately. People can give you words from God or what they think God may be saying to you, but in the end, hearing from Him is your responsibility. Receiving

---

9   John 2:5

feedback from the wrong people can confuse things significantly, and receiving from the right people can be a real blessing. Figuring out which is which before you talk to them is tricky, but ultimately none of them can replace you hearing from God for yourself and then acting in obedience.

GOING UNDER THE KNIFE

Our church in Tulsa gave us three options, only one of which we felt was the right one for us. From that, some people could be confused and think that we were at odds with our pastors, but, in fact, they prayed for us, contributed financially, sent us off with their blessing, and provided a great opportunity to solidify our decision to follow through on what God had said. When we first told them, their response was very practical; later it was very supportive. However, without the opportunities they presented, Lissa and I may not have been as clear about what God was telling us to do.

If you never encounter any difficulties (which can often take the form of either opportunity or opposition), your faith and commitment to God will never be tested. And if something is untested, you really don't know if it's real. Throughout the Bible, God tested His people in various ways. Abraham faced one of the most horrible tests imaginable—God told him to kill Isaac, the promised son God had given him—as a sacrifice. And he was going to do it. The knife was literally in the air, about to come down . . .

That's when God provided—right there with the knife in the air. We read that Abraham was willing to sacrifice his only son because he reasoned that if Isaac died, God was able to bring him back to life again.[10]

Sometimes God's tests will take you right to the edge—and

---

10   Hebrews 11:17-19

sometimes *right over* what you think of as the edge. But until you get to that precipice, until you're willing to have your knife out, willing to sacrifice your dream to obey God, you won't know if your faith is real.

God has taken us to the edge . . and beyond. Mongolia went off the edge of the map, into the Wilds far beyond the Shire. He took us farther than we'd ever dreamed we could go, and we were not the same when we returned. You will never know what He wants you to become until you step off the edge and into His arms.

HARD WORK BEGINS

We had about six months to raise $40,000. I had no job, no significant fundraising experience, and I had never run more than a marathon in my life. However, there's a saying I really love: "Opportunity is missed by most people because it's dressed in overalls and looks like hard work." (Now obviously, I don't mean "opportunity" as in the kind that distracts you from God's will!)

So I got busy.

Lissa, the detail person in the family, stayed with her part-time job at the church longer than I did. One of the implications of this was that she recognized that a lot of the responsibility for the planning was actually on me. We decided that preparing for the trip was my full-time job since I was no longer traditionally employed. She made the somewhat questionable decision to let me handle a ton of details.

I won't get into all of the fundraising, planning, training, and other things that occupied my time, but I do want to talk about how we planned the route and estimated how long it would take me to run across the entire country.

SPITBALLING

Lissa and I opened up an old-school paper map and laid it out on the floor, and then we both lay down on the floor to look at it. It was the first time that Lissa had even looked at a map of Mongolia. We had been saying "fifteen hundred miles" for some time, but seeing it on a map made a very different impression on her—on both of us, really.

"What do we need to do?" she asked.

I had my handy-dandy ruler out to measure distances on the map. "I guess we pick a road," I said hardly convincingly. "God said 'across,' so let's go west to east." We proceeded to lay out a course that followed major roads of Mongolia. (At this point, I didn't know that the major "road" across Mongolia was little more than a collection of dirt tracts running parallel across most of the country.)

I called out distances and measured with a ruler while Lissa tapped on her calculator. When we had all the miles added up, we had 1,503 miles between the major points connected by roads.

"How many miles can you run in a day?" she asked.

I honestly had no idea. "Thirty?" I replied. For some reason, there was never really another number that came to our minds. For some reason, that didn't come off as completely absurd and ridiculous at the moment. More than a marathon *per day*?

Using our easy, round number of miles a day in the distance across Mongolia, we estimated it would take fifty-six running days, with a few days factored in for me to ramp up to thirty, and one day a week to rest. We then looked at the calendar, guessed when we would land, decided how long we wanted to stay in the capital with the orphans, and penciled in a departure date to head back to the States.

Our spitball figuring had us done by September 19, 2013 at noon. We wanted to give ourselves a little flexibility, so we booked a ticket to fly out from the border town on September 20th.

There is no natural way that any human-made plans, let alone ones as haphazard and informal as the ones we made, should have worked out this precisely. The trip itself was improbable to say the least, but for some reason, just the simple timing of it all stands out to me as being a scheduling miracle all its own.

Earlier in the book, I mentioned that God does not owe us answers when we ask Him *why* and *how*. I told you that He likes to handle the details, and this is a perfect example to me. I have no other explanation for how our roughly estimated plans could possibly come together so accurately other than God being in charge of the details.

You may be looking at the imposing nature of what God is inspiring you to do. You may be sweating the details. Let me assure you, God is not sweating the details. He is not perturbed by schedules or timing, variables that He could forget to account for, or anything else. He knows what needs to happen and when.

In the aftermath of our own miracle experience (both the run and the timing of it all), it's become easy for me to tell you to let God worry about the details. God taught me something about them through this experience—they are His to worry about. Why worry about what is in God's wheelhouse? Can your worries do anything about it? They can no sooner turn a gray hair on your head back to the color nature intended than change any detail that is in God's court.[11]

I know it's hard to let them go. Believe me; I know! I can tell you now that God taught me to let them go and that you should do the same. Saying that is easy. Ceasing to worry is another matter entirely. In fact, I'd go so far as to say it's *impossible*.

I can tell you this: without His help, it's totally impossible to trust God. Letting go like that just isn't possible for most people. Although some have a gift for boundless optimism and make it look easy, it's tempting to hate those people because they think it's so simple.

I know it's not simple; I know how hard it is. Everything worth

---

11   Luke 12:22-30

doing is—it's hard, it's worth it, and it's the only way across your Mongolia.

THE CHILDREN'S PLACE ORPHANAGE

With the hard work in full swing, we knew we needed to look for partners in Mongolia. We didn't know the first thing about how practically to help the orphans in Ulaanbaatar. I can remember lying in bed late one night; next to me, Lissa's face was lit up by the glow of her computer screen as she searched for organizations that could partner with us.

We had no desire to try to reinvent the wheel or do something on our own, so we were looking for a group to strategically partner with that was already working with the children. We didn't want an organization that was too big, where the money we raised would get diluted by administration costs, but we didn't want one that was too small and wouldn't be able to handle the money appropriately.

Finally, after hours of clicking, Children's Place Mongolia captured Lissa's attention. She happened to see a phone number, so she impulsively picked up the phone and dialed. We didn't even know what time it was over there!

A woman answered the phone (it was midmorning there), and Lissa just said, "Hello, my name is Lissa Hunter. Do you speak English?" The woman on the other end said something, and the next thing she knew, it the voice of an American woman saying, "Hello?"

That was it—the floodgates opened, and Lissa started telling her what we wanted to do. The woman, Dr. Rita, got really excited about the possibility of partnering with us, and she and Lissa hit it off right away. But wait, this impromptu conversation got even better.

Dr. Rita started telling Lissa her backstory, including how she had come from Atlanta, Georgia. Suddenly Lissa interjected, "Our old pastor is from Atlanta." Dr. Rita asked his name, and Lissa answered, "Mike Atkins."

I can only imagine Dr. Rita's face when she heard that. In total surprise, she said, "He was my pastor!"

Mike (Pastor Mike from Jackson Hole) has been a mentor to us from the beginning—it was his church I had been "tricked" into going to years before. So to randomly make a connection with a woman on the other side of the world whom he had also touched was nothing short of miraculous!

We took little God moments like this as confirmation that we were on the right track, and that "Peace River" I told you about earlier flowed even more strongly as we made arrangements to partner with an organization halfway across the world that we felt connected to from the start because of Pastor Mike.

The orphanage provided long-term, sustainable care for twenty children elementary age through fifteen years old. From citizens who found the babies who had been abandoned to working with the police, the orphanage had stepped up to help save children from a horrible fate at the dumps. These lucky children went to school during the day but ate, slept, and lived at the orphanage, where caring adults looked after them. (We would later learn that this was the kind of life that the kids at the dump would die to have!)

We immediately found out what the money we raised could help with at the orphanage—at the top of the list was a new heating system. As I've mentioned, Ulaanbaatar is the coldest capital city in the world. The orphanage's heating unit was out of date and not working, and in Ulaanbaatar, if you don't have heat, you're in great danger. They also needed a new cooking range so that they could more efficiently cook for all the kids, and they needed some renovations to a playground area. Basically, the playground consisted of rocks and sticks and other junk, including broken glass and rusty nails.

Helping the orphanage was good, but we were yet missing a piece of the puzzle. The most weighty burden on our hearts was for the orphans at the city dump. We had yet to find an organization that would help us reach those kids, and in fact we wouldn't actually get connected until we arrived in Mongolia for a quick scouting mission.

MOTIVATION

This is a good time to revisit something I have mentioned before. Finding out about the orphanage's needs was great, but interestingly it was not what motivated me to get out of bed in the morning—or to do another mile on tough days while we were there. The benefit was for the kids, and, of course, the kids were a huge part of all this. However, for me the motivation was actually more about saying yes to what God wanted and looking forward to how He was going to solve the challenges each day brought.

If you've made it this far with me, you may understand why this was the case. While it may not seem particularly humanitarian of me, I want you to think for just a moment about goals. What happens when we accomplish a particular goal? We may feel a sense of accomplishment, but we also often feel strangely let down.

After summiting the mountain, what's left?

If your primary concern is not the immediate goal but the Person, the milestone is just a great place marker on the journey—the real adventure is your relationship with God.

Take just a moment to think about what motivates you. If you have a Mongolian-size dream in front of you, be really honest with yourself. Because if that is your end goal, you're still going to have to deal with life after you've accomplished it. However, if God is your goal, the memories you collect as mementos from your journey will fuel faith for future endeavors.

If it were all about Mongolia, if it were all about the kids, when I was done helping, I would just be a man who had helped some orphans and had run a lot of miles. But if it were about God, and through me God did a miraculous thing, then I can trust Him for the next big adventure. He gets the glory, He accomplishes the goal through me.

What do I get out of it?

I get to become a dangerous person, but I wouldn't find my identity.

CHAPTER 9

A LAND FORGOTTEN BY TIME

Do the difficult things while they are easy, and do the great things while they are small. A journey of a thousand miles must begin with a single step.

– Lao Tzu

Running across Mongolia and helping the orphans would not help me find my identity. In the period of intense training leading up to the run, I spent a lot of time with some ultra-long distance runners. Hearing of my plans, they warmly welcomed me into their tribe as one of their own. The problem was I had never really identified myself as a "runner" (and now even having run fifteen hundred miles across Mongolia, I still don't!). This made me an enigma to them because I did not define myself by the goal or the means of accomplishing it.

When I lived in Jackson Hole, Wyoming, I had the opportunity to mentor a young man named AJ who went on to graduate from the Naval Academy and then go straight into BUD/S[12] training to become a Navy SEAL. When he invited me to go out to California for his graduation, I eagerly accepted. I'm a huge fan of the super warriors the Navy SEAL program turns out, and as I arrived at the Naval Special Warfare Center, I was as giddy as a preteen girl at a boy-band concert.

The AJ I knew and had mentored wasn't there to meet me; someone else was. Someone stronger, more confident, and infinitely more dangerous had replaced him. AJ offered me a tour through the BUDs training compound, and while I kept cool on the outside, it was like that preteen girl was getting a backstage pass to meet her idol. As he walked me through the infamous O course, I asked him how he was different now that he was becoming a real-life superhero.

Despite how he had obviously changed, his answer surprised me: "I'm no different. I'm still just AJ. Being a SEAL is just my job; it's not who I am." With that statement, I began to realize just how strong AJ really had become. Despite having accomplished something that for many people i impossible, he had a stronger picture of who he really was than the dentity the elite US Navy SEAL's program could offer him. I'll never forget the conversation we shared as we walked through the soft sand, up, over, and through some of the different obstacle-course elements. I found myself being as proud of him as I have been of nearly anyone in my life.

BASICS TRAINING

Training didn't provide my identity, but it did take up a lot of my time.

I was all about three things for the next six months: fundraising, training, and logistics. I sent out emails to every outdoor-gear

12   Basic Underwater Demolition/SEAL

manufacturer on the planet, and a few were interested in helping. One, Right Socks™, was absolutely amazing and donated a fresh pair of running socks for every day I would be running! These double-layer socks were priceless for preventing blisters. Before I found these socks, I couldn't run five miles without getting a blister. And, after all the miles running in Mongolia, I only had one blister ever! This one company felt like a bright ray of sunshine on a stormy day because it was very encouraging to know that someone believed in what we were doing.

For all you athletes out there, here's what my training regimen looked like. I ran eight-to-ten miles five days a week, did a long run of fifteen miles or more once a week, and sprinkled in some CrossFit workouts three or four days a week. I had never been in such great shape in my entire life! But there's a fine line between training to boost conditioning, and overtraining and getting injured before you even set out. My single biggest week, I ran twenty miles a day for five straight days—and I thought I was going to *die*.

But I don't want this book to be about how to train to run across Mongolia. Let's just leave it at this—this worked for me, unorthodox though it may have been, but results may vary. I had other fish to fry besides just training.

I also had to plan the expedition side, and for this I fell back on my hiking and camping experience. I knew what I'd needed for multi-day outings, so I had a framework for the supplies we'd need. I just expanded the scope for the weeks we'd be on the trail. We bought a ton of supplies to take with us—things we knew we couldn't get over there—and we re-supplied the other items as we went.

It turns out that the biggest costs would be transportation—to country and within the country—and food. Alone, I'd need five-to-seven thousand calories a day. What I didn't know was that Mongolian cooking looks nothing like Genghis Grill™ or HuHot™ and that by the last third of the trip, my appetite would kind of give out on the bland Mongolian diet, despite our cook's best efforts.

The most precious commodities we brought with us were Nutella(tm)- and peanut butter—two indispensable daily calorie fillers we couldn't get in Asia. Of the 400 pounds of gear we brought with us, at least 250 was food we'd purchased in bulk. (Another minor miracle—Lissa cleaned out our *last* jars of peanut butter and Nutella™ to make sandwiches on the *last* day of running for the *last* ten miles.)

The language barrier and radical time difference made logistical planning challenging with our Mongolian contacts. Remember how I said that saying yes to God was the hardest part? Well, I think something in us thought that after committing-to-God's-adventure-for-us, everything else would be, well, easy. Be assured, it was not. But time and time again, God showed us that doing things His way may not make sense to us—but it's the only way to accomplish His mission.

During my planning, I made an important connection—Tulga, who was to be known as our fixer. Tulga is a no-nonsense kind of guy. He'd been to the States a few times, and his English was quite good. He was our make-it-happen guy. He lined up our two drivers and a cook, Duya.

UNPREDICTABLE BUT DEPENDABLE

A story from the Bible recounts the Israelites doing some strange things to obey God. First, they're out of water, which is really bad in the Middle East. And then they're about to be attacked by not one but three enemy armies, so they inquire of God what they should do. What battle plan does God's prophet share with them? Does He give them unparalleled tactical genius?

No, he tells them to dig ditches—in the middle of the desert.

And you know they're wondering how in the world wasting what strength they have left digging a bunch of ditches is going to help them with their enemies. But God had a plan, and He was living up to His reputation.

Though always faithful and dependable, God can often be unpredictable. And, quite frankly, we hate that. We want to understand. We want to know the how and the why, but God isn't too interested in those items, as we've covered. He is into making His name famous.

So the story plays out—they bake away in the sun, with no water, digging ditches as their enemies close in. They fall into exhausted sleep, thinking one way or another—through thirst or by the sword—they're going to die in the very near future.

But they wake up to find that the ditches they dug the day before have filled with water. And not just that, but their enemies see the red sunrise reflected off the water, and they think that it is blood from a great battle. So they rush down to collect the plunder from the battle, but the men of Israel are waiting to attack, and the Israelites win a great victory.

I imagine that this is not how the leaders of Israel envisioned victory over their enemies. It required a pretty huge step of faith to trust what God told them to do—dig ditches in the desert—which I'm pretty sure made about as much sense to them as it would to us (maybe about as much sense as running across Mongolia).

So why tell you about this somewhat-obscure miracle God did for His people in the desert? Because it illustrates that what God tells us may not make much sense, and His faithfulness may seem unpredictable—we often won't understand what He's up to. But in the final analysis, He is always dependable.

God will give us a vision—a mission. But we must be willing to submit to the calling and have faith, even when it makes no human sense. He often asks us to do the hard work to make that vision a reality before we have understanding. He will use our effort done in faith as a conduit to transfer His provision to us, and in so doing, we will accomplish more than we ever could on our own. Ultimately, in the end, He gets all the credit.

In our world, this looked like running across Mongolia—that was the vision. We had to buy in, put our yes on the table, and agree to do it. The hard work was all the prep and planning, and the running too.

Even how we raised the money didn't fit our expectations. We prayed because we didn't know what to do, and God gave us several ideas. Some were simple, and others were mind-blowing ideas we never would've thought up on our own. They were God's ideas.

However—and this might pop some bubbles—even God ideas take hard work. One idea was making custom, country-style kitchen tables. We raised thousands of dollars, and while God provided for us that way, it was not money simply raining from the heavens. It took hard work.

Do you have a vision for a "Mongolia" in your life? Awesome! Get ready for some hard work—and be prepared for God to go about it in unexpected (but always faithful) ways. It may be time to dig some ditches.

CHAPTER 10

THE ROAD LESS TRAVELED

---

*I have found that there are three stages in every great work of God:
first, it is impossible, then it is difficult, then it is done.*

– Hudson Taylor

We were almost ready to head out, and all the months of preparation were going to culminate in a trip to Mongolia, which may or
may not be physically disastrous. About three weeks before we were
scheduled to leave for Mongolia, I visited the dentist for a regular
checkup, and he found a cavity that required a root canal—a two-day
root canal!

Now, I don't want to whine because many of us have had root canals
over the years, but I found that I couldn't train after the root canal
because of the pain. In fact, I was down about five days. And then to
add insult to injury, I developed a very bad infection and got really

sick. Five days of antibiotics temporarily beat the infection down, but less than a week after I stopped antibiotics, the fever and infection were back again. It came down to the question of whether to try more antibiotics and see how that works, or pull the tooth. By now, I had very little time to heal before my trip to third-world country.

The tooth had to go.

I like to say now that Mongolia cost me a tooth. The day after my dentist pulled the tooth, I felt a lot better, but the whole experience had cost me a lot. I had put on about ten pounds of muscle during my training, but while I was so sick, I lost all that weight—muscles and reserves. I now did not have enough time to put the weight back on before we left, but I had to get back to training. I tried training a few miles on a bike, but then I realized that riding the bike uses different muscles than running. And finally, somehow while stretching my ankle and calf, I injured a ligament in my ankle on the inside of my right foot—three days before we were going to leave! My jaw hurt, and I couldn't put weight on my ankle. Apparently, I was done training even though I was supposed to run fifteen hundred miles starting in just a few days.

Let's just say that I could think of better ways to start. It's tempting to think that if a dream is from God, He will pave the way before you. I'm reminded of the scene from the movie *Bruce Almighty* where he has just gained divine powers and parts the traffic before him like Moses parting the Red Sea. That's what we want—we want God to use His divine powers to make the path before us easy.

But how do we handle setbacks? How do we handle it when it isn't easy? Just because it's God doesn't mean that the path before us will be simple or uncomplicated or easy.

It starts with commitment. Lissa and I had put our yeses to God firmly on the table, so a sprained ankle and hole in my jaw wasn't going to deter us. If I had to hobble on crutches for the first two weeks before I could run, that's what we were going to do.

However, that doesn't mean I was *comfortable*—a "god" we so often seek to serve. In the modern pantheon, we have Lord Comfort and Lady Convenience to follow, but it was the fear of the Lord and the fact that I was motivated by a desire to serve God above all else that helped me push through.

CHINESE DRESS-CODE ISSUES

So I spent the days before we left lounging around the house, popping ibuprofen, and eating with my foot propped up. Amazingly, the hardest days on my ankle were actually while we traveled— standing in long lines at the airports, getting through customs, and all the rest of the standing that happens while traveling. I was okay if I could sit down, and I must admit that my thoughts were a constant litany of doubts: *If I can't even stand on it, how am I going to be able to run on it?* And my familiar chorus of: *You're too old, you're too late, and you'll never succeed.*

We had one other "fun" setback just getting to Mongolia involving Chinese airlines. A friend of ours, an American Airlines pilot, helped us get flights into Beijing, but from there we had to buy regular tickets to get to Ulaanbaatar (which we should have already purchased). However, the ticket agent needed to see that we had a round-trip ticket purchased for *leaving* China, and if they didn't see that we had a flight itinerary departing China, they wouldn't let us leave.

We arrived four hours early for our flight, had done all the preparation and fundraising to get to this point, pushed through the setbacks, and now we could not board the plane! However, by this point Lissa and I had grown quite accustomed to working with a narrow margin of possibility. We were no longer looking for easy or even likely; we just needed a sliver of possibility, and we would push through that crack.

So without blinking an eye, my lioness says, "So what do we need in order to go?" Turns out we either needed a visa from the Chinese Embassy (in Chicago) or proof of a round-trip ticket. The budget didn't account for the second option, but we had benefactors. Lissa's parents ended up using their SkyMiles™ to buy all four of us round-trip tickets to Beijing—tickets that we didn't even use because we only had them for the sake of our itinerary.

But the Chinese were not done with us yet. We then found out we had to meet dress code. Many years ago when flying was still a novelty, people actually dressed up to fly. I know this is a novel concept to a generation who thinks that the designer t-shirt and skinny jeans qualifies as "dressing up," but once upon a time, one had to wear a blazer and business attire to fly. Things haven't changed much in certain parts of the world, and much to my irritation, I discovered that apparently my shoes were not up to code.

"Sir, you can't get on the plane with those shoes," I was told. "They are not the appropriate dress code."

Lissa just about exploded. After all we'd been through, our trip was now being threatened by a wardrobe malfunction? I told her, "Get on the plane, and stall. Don't let them leave!"

So as my family went down the jetway, I tried to work with the uncooperative gate agent of the Chinese airlines. He suggested a change of shoes, but I did not have any other shoes with me; neither was there a store nearby where I could buy a different pair. In desperation, I tried to break the language barrier with passersby by asking them to trade shoes, which had predictably negative results. Finally, after pleading my case, the gate agent finally said, "Hold on, let me check."

He was gone ten minutes, but it felt like much longer. Would he come back? I didn't know. All the other passengers already boarded the plane. I couldn't help but think of the irony that I wouldn't be able to run across Mongolia because I couldn't even get into the country because of my stinking shoes.

But he finally did come back, and I waited with bated breath for him to tell me my fate.

"Okay, Sir, you can go," he said.

We were on our way to Beijing!

We had more adventures just getting there, including our flight into Ulaanbaatar, which was unable to land because of high winds. We didn't know that at the time, of course, since all the comments from the pilot were in Mandarin. Finally a fellow passenger told us what was going on in broken English: "No land in Ulaanbaatar. We go back to Beijing, try tomorrow."

On our third day of international travel, we dragged ourselves into Ulaanbaatar. The kids were just fried, and Lissa and I weren't much better. Tulga, our fixer, met us at the airport (a *fixer* is the person from your host country that makes everything work—he's the go-to man, the make-it-happen guy. He spoke decent English and is probably one of the more well-connected men in his country). So with a final push through the expedition's logistics, an interview on Mongolian TV, and a trip through customs, we were almost ready to start the "hard" part—the running.

LANDING IN MONGOLIA

Ulaanbaatar, the Mongolian capital, is a big city, even if it is not a Western one. As I mentioned, a huge percentage of the population of the country actually lives in the capital, so it is a busy Asian metropolis with some of the familiar hallmarks of any big city.

Tulga put us up in a little hostel for our brief stay in the capital before we headed out. We had a large enough group that we got our own room at the hostel, so we didn't have to share space with travelers from around the world preparing to trek through the Gobi or ride a camel.

Lissa was focused on the kids we were there to help. I admit, that is probably a more noble focus than I had for this part of the trip. Since I'd hurt my ankle just shortly before we were to leave, most of my attention was on the fact that only days after arriving in Mongolia, I would be putting thirty miles a day on the same ankle I currently had elevated and iced.

We had sent the money we had raised on ahead of us to the orphanage; we didn't want to run the risk of something happening while transporting that kind of cash. We would also be using funds to help an outreach at the city dump, which was a far more desperate need. We actually raised more money as the trip went on, but even before I took a step, we had already accomplished one of the most important goals by getting financial provision to some people who desperately needed it.

Children's Place Mongolia, the orphanage, was ready for us when we arrived, and they had planned a performance for us! My kids, shyly hiding behind our legs, were nervous about meeting their first Mongolian children, but the orphanage director led us to the well-lit basement, which was full of bright, happy, cheerful children, and quickly we saw how happy these kids were to see us—and it was infectious! We loved the energy, life, and bright colors—and the sense of hope! These adorable children sang, did skits, and did little dance numbers—all in Mongolian—to entertain us. Afterwards, we gave our kids some bubbles to blow for our new friends, and this combined with having just seen their show melted away the nervousness as the universal language of "fun" crossed cultural borders.

One of the things that is so special about this orphanage is that it has kids with special needs, and it has trained workers to help them. Not only does the orphanage provide basic care for orphans, they act as a rehabilitation center for special-needs kids. Parents of special-needs kids can bring their children to the center, and they themselves are trained and given resources to help raise their children to thrive despite their disabilities.

While not as much a "death sentence" as our Western American imaginations might think, Mongolia generally lacks the knowledge and resources to handle special-needs children. This makes their quality of life much lower for the kids and much harder on the parents than in a Western nation. We were so glad to be able to partner with an organization doing such a great service.

All this provided laser focus on exactly why God had us there, and it provided fuel for me as I ran. On the flip side, it actually made it a little harder too. Normally one would get money after accomplishing a task; here, we had already given most of the money away before I ever ran a mile!

It all got very real when we said goodbye to the kids and boarded a plane from Ulaanbaatar to Ulgee. Where is that, you ask?

The middle of nowhere!

FRIGHTENED BY THE VIEW

When we flew into Ulgee on a small commercial prop plane, I was staring out the window at the countryside, trying to get an idea of the ground over which I would be running very shortly. The countryside from an altitude of a few thousand feet was stark and barren, desolate, with no signs of civilization. Ulgee is on the western edge of Mongolia, and in a short few hours, we flew over the whole lot of nothing that I would spend the next two and a half months of my life running across.

It was now my time to make my contribution to this expedition—

quite simply, run thirty a day, every day, until we reached the far eastern border of Mongolia where it touches China. I was really freaking out on the plane ride, thinking of my ankle and the gaping hole in my jaw where my tongue kept expecting to find a tooth. I felt woefully inadequate to the task we flew over, and I was scared to death of what I had gotten myself and my family into. Had I really heard God? We were about to find out.

TOO FAR TO BACK OUT NOW

Panic, despair, and the weight of what we were about to do threatened to pull the plane out of the sky as we flew the hour and a half to Ulgee. I was just about crushed under this weight of responsibility. I was sweating, and my stomach was tied up in knots. For all these months, it had been just an exercise—planning for an outreach. But now . . . now, I would really have to run across Mongolia. Many people had helped get us here, but now it was time for me to deliver. I was not at all sure I could. It was daunting to say the least.

You've probably heard before that we often lack perspective on our problems, that we need a "big-picture" view. Some people use altitude terms like we need "the 30,000-foot view." The thinking here is that from a height, our problems can often look very small.

That works well . . . until it only makes things worse! Flying over the vastness of Mongolia, the big-picture view was making me ready to throw up. For me, seeing the issue at hand—running across a country—from the air only exacerbated my concerns and worries.

But I had been in this place many times before (not geographically but metaphorically). Remember, I'm famous for biting off more than I can chew, for instance in a mountain adventure. I have a well-rehearsed routine for when it's too late to back out.

I suck it up, take my first step, and then hope that no one notices that my knees are knocking together in fear. Even if I can't fool myself, I know by putting on a brave show and just taking the next step, I can trick the rest of the world into thinking I'm the model of confidence and preparedness.

I felt like a paratrooper during the invasion of Normandy, dropping into enemy-held territory. The light is green, and the only thing left to do is cinch my helmet tight and jump.

A PLAGUE OF FLIES

No one worked at the airport in Ulgee—at least that's how it seemed. We looked around and didn't see workers as we exited the plane straight to the tarmac in the early summer Mongolian heat. Other than the lack of workers, the first thing we noticed were these small flies that were *everywhere*.

There were swarms of them, and they got in everything! It was like we were reliving the book of Exodus just in time for God to hit Mongolia with a biblical plague. Our vehicles had not arrived yet to pick us up, so we and all of our supplies had nowhere to go to escape the heat and the flies, including inside the airport, which was not air conditioned nor a defense against the flies.

"What have we gotten ourselves into?" Lissa asked breathlessly. We were certainly both thinking it.

This was the start of a new philosophy: *Shut your mouth, and don't you dare complain.*

But wait; it gets better! Just as we're arriving, a Land Cruiser™ races up, and a team is getting a man on a stretcher on board the airplane we had just left. He's a Westerner, and he looks bad. In need of medical attention that he can't get out in the middle of nowhere, he's getting on the Mongolian equivalent of a Life Flight™ for the medical attention he can receive in the capital. His head was all bandaged up, and he was unresponsive.

We watched him with wide eyes. This was the thought going through my mind: *This is an example of what Mongolia can do to us soft Westerners—chew them up and spit them out.* I couldn't help but wonder what the country had in store for me and my family.

THE CREW

Eventually our drivers showed up—fifty-something EK in a 1970s-era, ubiquitous-to-Mongolia, indestructible Russian military van; and a young guy named Venus in a Lexus GX 470 (basically a fancy Toyota Land Cruiser™). Along with Tulga and Duya, the cook, they were our Mongolian support team. It took about two hours to load our several-hundred pounds of gear into and onto the support vehicles for the very first time. After we had everything situated and tied down, we pulled out of the airport and headed west for the border.

In addition to Tulga's support crew, we temporarily had a medic, Jason, who came with us from the States. Jason is an amazing guy and a fire paramedic—super qualified for any kind of medical emergency and well-equipped with a suitcase full of medical supplies. This was a great comfort as we would be far from medical help, except for the fact that he would only be with us for the first ten days.

Sure hope nothing goes wrong after that!

I thought that partially in jest. I realized that I couldn't carry the baggage of my fears off the plane with me. I knew I couldn't do the job I had to do under that weight. I know you're not supposed to leave your baggage on the plane when you get off, but I was glad to leave that stuff behind. Whatever challenges lay ahead, I would tackle them one at a time.

I simply prayed, "God, help." I brought to mind all the miraculous things He had done that had led up to this moment. So many things He had done to just get us this far had been minor miracles themselves.

So I made a conscious effort to delete those things—the worries, doubts, and insecurities—from my brain. Crippling fears didn't step off with me. (I just hope they weren't waiting for the passengers that got on for the flight back.)

CHAPTER 11

THE ONLY EASY DAY WAS YESTERDAY

It pays to be a winner.
– a Navy SEAL saying

Though I had dealt with the intense fears and insecurities on the flight to Ulgee, opportunities for new concerns were easy to come by. I tried not to think about losing our medic or the Westerner being air-lifted out as we got started with the one-hundred-kilometer drive out to the border, which provided our first really good chance to get a ground-level look at the lay of the land. The first thing I noticed is that one can see from horizon to horizon. At night, the entire sky is a vast dome, the bright and star-filled strip of the Milky Way bisecting the heavens from one side to another. During the day, there's little or nothing to interrupt your view—Montana has nothing on Mongolia for the title of Big Sky Country.

Mongolia is very cold in the winter due to its latitude and altitude (remember, Ulaanbaatar is the coldest capital in the world with an average temperature of 32 degrees Fahrenheit), but despite long, frigid winters, the short summers are hot. The Gobi Desert occupies the south, but most of the land is what's called steppes—large, dry grasslands with very few trees. A lot of the country is this arid range of dirt and pockets of vegetation that don't have enough green to even support marmots. So this desert-like climate is cold at night and in the 90s or more during the day.

Our new family mandate of not complaining kept our mouths shut, but we drove with wide eyes, wondering what Mongolia might have in store for us. I learned right then that we could not look too far ahead. We had to take it one day at a time. This is actually a very good life lesson: no matter if we are literally in the middle of nowhere or navigating a crowded urban jungle, worrying about tomorrow gets us nowhere; staying in the present and rooted in God's promises, taking it one day at a time, is the only way to get through.

Lissa had made a calendar that featured July, August, and September in big blocks out of duct tape to put up in our brand-new tent. We set up camp beside a lake for that first leg of the run, and for the first few days, the calendar was displayed proudly as she kept careful track of our progress. But in less than a month, the duct-tape calendar was rolled up and set aside as a piece of memorabilia. We simply couldn't look at our trip in terms of crossing off days until the goal. We just had to look at what each day's challenges presented.

INSANE ROADS

When I mention roads in Mongolia, you may be thinking of paved highways or even Route 66, a bit run down but serviceable. But in Mongolia, we followed the main artery across the country, but let me tell you, that's not saying much. Mongolian roads are impossible to travel without four-wheel-drive. All but a few miles of roads around the capital are dirt, but not just dirt, I'm talking two-track roads made by tires rolling over the scrubby vegetation.

Over and over, Lissa and I found ourselves saying we couldn't believe this was the main road. In most places, it was so rough that even four-wheel-drive vehicles could only go five or ten miles an hour.

Adding to the unique character of the country is that Mongolians are quite comfortable making their own new roads at any point in time. So if a road gets washed out or it gets too rutted or too rough, they have no problem going fifteen feet to the right or to the left and making a brand-new parallel road cutting across the steppes. Mongolia has only had the automobile for perhaps a generation, but that's long enough for seemingly every vehicle crossing the country to have made its own little two-track road through the countryside.

The real issue here is that gradually the roads have grown wider, with paths switching back and forth among the two-tracks, creating a braided network of parallel paths all in the same direction but separated by enough distance that it created a problem for us. In following the support vehicles, how would I know which track they had taken?

FIRST DAY OF RUNNING

We made our first camp in Mongolia by the shores of picturesque White Lake. Our spirits had rebounded from the scare we had upon landing, as working out new and shiny gear can do. At this point, we had been traveling for nearly four days, but finally the effort to get in country was over, and it was time to actually do what we came here for.

Our first Mongolian visitor drove up to our camp on a motorcycle, a baby tucked into the front of his jacket and a boy about my son,

Kai's, age behind him. The kids proceeded to kick a soccer ball around by the lake, and life felt just great. That first day, I was able to forget about the running and the miles and simply camp with family and new friends.

The next day we headed out to the border with a plan of gradually ramping up to thirty miles a day to "give my ankle a chance to heal." My goal for the first day was to run from the Russian border back to camp, which was about fifteen miles.

At the border between Mongolia and Russia, you are as far west as you can go and still be in Mongolia. We had to get permission to approach the border, but our accompanying Mongolian border patrol agent brought us very close. "Do you see the white post?" he asked us (through Tulga, our translator). "If you go past this post, the Russian border guard will shoot you."

I wasn't sure I believed him, but I wasn't about to test it. From a safe distance, we took pictures and knelt together to pray. At this point, I wasn't scared anymore. In fact, I was giddy like a schoolgirl! After we prayed, everyone clapped and cheered as I headed off back toward camp. I set off on my journey east, feeling just like Frodo bearing the Ring of Power.

I got a little taste of a variety of Mongolian weather that first day running with a bit of rain before the sun came out. But right away, I also encountered my first challenge of finding a route. I knew our campsite was on the lake, just past the mountain, but I was not sure which side of the mountain. With very few roads and easy terrain, you could just kind of drive where you wanted, so there was no road to follow.

I ran around the close side of the mountain and didn't see our camp or the big lake. That meant they must be on the other side, so I backtracked around the mountain. I had already run about fifteen miles, which was the most mileage I had wanted to do as a warm-up run on the first day. But Mongolia was introducing me to the hardship I was to expect for the rest of the expedition. Some twenty miles later, I found my way around the other side of the mountain and back to camp.

By the end of that first day, my jaw was throbbing, but my ankle felt surprisingly good while running. Turns out, standing on it in line was far worse than running on it. As I trotted into camp that first day, I thought of the Navy SEAL saying, "The only easy day was yesterday," and I shuttered to think of the hundreds and hundreds of miles that lay ahead.

MEET THE GERR FAMILY

A couple days into the run, I found myself in a large, glacier-scoured valley. I was running next to a beautiful little stream, and I had already put on about fifteen miles for the day. That might sound like beautiful scenery, but it was actually very barren—no trees, very little vegetation. But every now and then I could see these little gerrs, traditional Mongolian huts or tents. The gerrs are made from layers of wool from sheep and goat hair. A vinyl-tarp-outer layer that they can peel back lets the inside of the tent breathe.

As I was running along, a group of children and one older girl strayed from their gerrs to come see what the crazy Westerner was doing. I to this day do not speak more than a few words of Mongolian, but these happy children (who looked more like they were from Afghanistan or Kazakhstan) were very excited to meet me. Through pantomime and hand gestures, I tried to convey that I was running across Mongolia. They couldn't believe it, and with a smile and a wave, I trotted off down the road having made my first Mongolian friends on my own. I remember thinking how cool it would be if my family could meet this little family.

At the end of my miles that day, the support vehicle picked me up to take me back to camp. Next day we would be moving camp, and I would have to drive right past these people to pick up my miles. So I asked Tulga if we could stop and visit with them the next day. I couldn't wait to try to visit with our first real nomadic Mongolian family.

He agreed, and the next day we stopped outside their little collection of tents. Tulga got out to talk with the patriarch of the family, and when he came back, Tulga said, "It's okay. He welcomes you." We happily piled out of the car, and I had a chance to shake hands with the patriarch.

A little girl about the same age as my daughter came up, grabbed Selah's hand, and took off running. My son headed off after them, tearing full speed into the Mongolian countryside. The weather was gorgeous, the sun shining down on this broad valley where the family lived in the middle of nowhere. A rambunctious stream wound its way through the valley, which was almost a mile wide and devoid of most vegetation. The valley floor and surrounding hillsides were a mass of jumbled loose rock and scree. The only green one could see amid the sea of rock was the little island of lush green grass where the gerrs were set up, green grass and white gerr tents standing in sharp contrast to the monochromatic grey backdrop of the surrounding talus-strewn hillsides.

We just took a break, sitting on the cool grass and letting the kids play as we got to know a little bit about this Mongolian family. Jason, our medic, and Venus, one of the drivers, started up an impromptu wrestling match—wrestling is huge over there—which was probably the highlight of our visit for this family. Clean, well-groomed children cheered them on loudly. (I found it interesting that the kids had messy and worn clothes, but they were like the play clothes of kids anywhere, and the kids were happy and not dirty. This was not what I had expected from people living a nomadic lifestyle.)

We also had the chance to meet one of the older daughters. She had actually graduated from a university in the capital with a degree in a highly technical field. However, her parents had wanted her to come back and live with them. So, a young woman with a college education in a highly technical field was living in tents, with no electricity, running water, or sanitation. Her story, a microcosm of the tale being told in many developing nations, is mind boggling to us, but this collision of two worlds goes on in many different countries, even our own.

It was so much fun when Lissa brought out her guitar and played for our new friends. Our team and our new Mongolian friends gathered around and sat in a big circle on the soft grass. I felt like we were the von Trapp family sitting at the feet of Maria in the Sound Of Music. Though they couldn't sing along, they clapped merrily with the music. Then she busted out a little box of harmonicas and played a quick tune, and everyone wanted to try these amazing new instruments.

It was about then that we looked around and noticed our kids were nowhere to be seen! It had been an hour and a half or more since we'd last seen them. We asked Tulga to inquire of our new friends, and the patriarch smiled and pointed off to the hillside. Sure enough, about a mile away on the opposite side of the valley, we could see Selah and Kai as little dots of color, with their new little friend, herding about two hundred goats into the valley.

As they came in, there was a frenzy of activity as the women tied up the goats by tying their necks together before milking the goats for the evening. Our kids got to herd goats and ride horses, so this great diversion was a win for everyone.

After perhaps three hours with our new friends, we said our good-byes and headed out. We all felt this incredible feeling, and I had new energy as I did my miles that day.

FRIENDS ALONG THE ROAD LESS TRAVELED

Among the interesting personalities we met during this early part of the trip was a young man hitchhiking his way around the world. We couldn't figure out if his name was Tim or Tom, so we ended up calling him Tim-Tom. On the same desolate road that we were on, Tim Tom was traveling from one of the Slavic nations—we never did figure out which—and he had made it all the way across western Russia in about four days before getting stuck for three days in the first hundred kilometers of Mongolia.

I share that as a story to illustrate how desolate Mongolia is and how few people inhabit it. Take a quick look at a map and how big Russia is; now consider that he crossed all of Western Russia in just four days, yet just getting one hundred kilometers through Mongolia had taken him three days. There was simply no one to hitch a ride from.

We ended up giving Tim-Tom a ride, and he was with us for about a day. He had no money, and our food was closely rationed, but we got him something to eat, helped him cover some miles, and then dropped him off at a "major" (for Mongolia) road junction near the town of Hovd and wished him well.

Another interesting person we came across was Jacob, a cyclist. It had been a really hot, flat section of road, but the team had found us a delightful campsite tucked into a pristine valley—one of the few times we saw trees the whole time. I invited Jacob to spend the night in our camp with us. As a fellow soldier of the long dusty road, I longed for some camaraderie.

Jacob was traveling light and simple—just his bike, a trailer, and his wits. He needed very few things to sustain his journey, and it made me feel that our expedition was large, slow, and cumbersome in comparison. Despite the miles we'd covered together that day, we talked long into the night about our travels, life, the universe, everything. Jacob shared our camp with us, and we ate and laughed in our meeting tent, a luxury Jacob's bike trailer didn't contain.

The next day we got up and had a very nice breakfast. He hopped on his bike and rode off down the valley on a beautiful single-track trail. I took a parallel route on the ridge top. As he rode off, I felt a sense of loss and missed him already. Even though we had only spent a total of about five hours conversing, I felt like we understood each other at a deep level. Even though my family had accompanied me for every mile, only Jacob knew the loneliness, pain, and suffering of traveling each of those miles under your own power.

I felt a deep sense of loneliness in an endless expanse of rugged wilderness. Like no one else, Jacob knew what kind of mind games the endless road ahead can play. He knew the oppression of withering heat, bone-soaking rain, and the bite of cold that could cut through any layers.

In a moment of loneliness, I broke down in tears and actually screamed out his name. I wanted him to turn around, to stop, for us to travel together just a few miles.

But he didn't stop. He was now just a speck of color far in the distance.

I strained my eyes to watch his progress until he was gone. The moment I could no longer see him, my strength gave out. I was hot, tired, my legs felt like lead, and my chest was tight from choking back tears that welled up in my eyes. I stopped running and sat down. While chewing on an energy bar that tasted like packed sawdust, I lay back in the grass with my arm draped over my face and had a good cry.

That sense of belonging, of shared experience, had quickly created a bond of friendship unexpectedly there on the Mongolian steppes. We crave that as people, but I did so then especially because of the extreme loneliness of my journey. I needed to be understood, to take strength from knowing that I wasn't alone.

Now it was just the road, God, and me again. Alone.

. . . And yet not so alone. I knew One, like Jacob, did understand. And God isn't such a poor companion that we should say to ourselves, "Well, it's only me and God now." I reminded myself that I wasn't with a God who couldn't understand me but One who sent His Son, Jesus, who lived and died as a Man, just like me. He gets it because if no one else could relate to what I was feeling, I knew Jesus understood what it's like to be alone.

He'd experienced at a deep level that I can't even imagine the pain we go through. God hadn't left us in our cold, dark pit of loneliness; He'd peered over the lip of the pit, left heaven, and became a Man so He could crawl down into our existence with us. After I had foolishly expended precious bodily fluid on tears (but now feeling a little better), I got up, dusted myself off, and jogged off down the trail leading east.

Always east.

THE REAL MONGOLIAN GRILL

One of the good things was that all the activity made our kids so hungry they'd eat just about anything put in front of them, but we quickly learned to not ask what kind of meat we were eating. Kai took a particular liking to what we called "horse pockets," little dumplings filled with, you guessed it, horse meat.

Breakfast was often what they called "children's rice," which was a Cream-of-Wheat™-kind of thing made with yak milk, usually fresh from the yak, and mixed with water and sugar. It wasn't that bad. Sometimes we could get a hold of bacon or, more rarely, eggs. Mongolia, an under-developed country, isn't big on chickens, so what might be considered an ubiquitous source of protein was hard to come by.

Because of the hard and rocky soil, Mongolia is not generally fertile, so the diet consists of a lot of noodles imported from Russia or China. The lamb that comprised a lot of our meat wasn't the tender, tasty kind we get in the States or from New Zealand—it had a really distinct, pungent odor, and over time, my appetite took a nosedive. For the last few weeks, I covered my thirty miles on maybe two thousand calories—and that was a good day. Most of the time I got less, but my body had become super- efficient, and I wasn't losing much weight.

SPIDER CAMP

It took us about a week to get from the Russian border to the first town, Hovt. Hot, dry, monochromatic landscapes had crawled by in a blur of dull, red-brown dust. And then suddenly we were overlooking the blue lake! Along with the water came the mosquitoes, so we ate dinner in the meeting tent with the screens zipped up.

We couldn't really be outside that afternoon or evening, so we just rushed to our tents—which was okay with me because I was utterly exhausted. I pulled off my shoes, hopped into the tent, and immediately crashed.

In the morning, I woke up looking at the upper half of our tent, which is all mesh. At the intersection of the tent poles, I saw a big, dark lump of something. Mold? No, it couldn't have grown so fast.

Every morning, it takes me a while just to be able to stand up, but as soon as I could, I stood up to examine whatever it was. I still couldn't tell, so I poked at it, and about a million spiders began to vibrate with motion. For a moment, I couldn't tell if they were inside the tent or outside it, which of course makes all the difference when you're talking about spiders.

Normally, spiders don't bother me all that much, but seeing countless numbers of them inches from my face and over my family was a different story. They started scurrying down the outside of the tent, and you could actually *hear* them! So, like some sort of crazed gorilla in a cage, I started shaking our tent to knock them off. By now the family was up, and let's just say Lissa didn't like this situation at all.

Eventually the flood of spiders ended, and with a lot of peering through the mesh, I eventually decided it was safe enough to venture outside. You remember how I told you that I learned my lesson about putting my boots outside the tent from my first hike through the Continental Divide? Well, apparently I'm a slow learner.

Slow learner or not, I do know enough to always shake my boots out before I put them on (in case there is a rattlesnake in there), and this is the procedure I observed with my running shoes as well. So I picked up my first shoe, and I tapped it out—at least two dozen spiders crawled out of my shoe.

They were everywhere—in every nook and cranny, in everyone's gear. Apparently they were harmless, but we all spent a lot of time shaking them out of our gear because no one likes spiders, harmless or not, camping out in our equipment.

When we tell that story to people, a lot of them freak out. In the zone we were in, we took it in stride, however, like my buddy Indiana Jones calmly knocking spiders off with a bull whip. At least they weren't the mammoth spider that Frodo and Sam had to face on their journey.

BY FAITH THROUGH GRACE

It was a particularly warm day just six days into the run. I was running along with what had become the status quo—the support vehicle would wait for me at about five-mile intervals. I had left camp that morning and was on mile two, and the support vehicle had gone on ahead and would meet me in about three miles.

So it was right about here, now that I was finally alone, that suddenly the weight of all the miles I had yet to run came crashing down on me. Basically, I still had the full fifteen-hundred miles yet to run. I'd hardly even scratched the surface.

I was exhausted. Already. And it was just mile two. Everything was sore, and I could not get my mind away from how many miles I had to go. I started to get scared. Could I do this?

Fear entered my mind in a big way.

The moment fear entered my mind and I let myself go there, I stopped running. I can't make it 1,500 miles, I thought. I can hardly go 2 today! I wasn't even sure how I was going to go 30 miles that day. And if I couldn't cover 30 miles that day, I had no idea how I would cover 100 miles or 300 miles in the weeks to come, let alone the full-length of Mongolia. I had yet, in fact, to cover the full 30 miles any day I had run.

Fear stopped me in my tracks. It completely stopped my forward momentum, and it completely colored my impression of the future.

If I weren't able to run thirty miles a day, which was required to accomplish our mission in the amount of time we had, I was so tired that I thought I might as well give up now.

I sat down on the side of the road in the dust. I'm done, I thought. I started to rationalize why I couldn't do it and what I would tell people. I didn't think the people at home would be mad at me for not finishing the run; I tried to convince myself that the important thing was that I had tried. No one important to me would beat me up over giving up on an impossible venture.

I was just done. I decided to wait for the support vehicle to realize I was overdue and to come get me. I didn't cry, even though I was emotionally exhausted. Nothing inside of me wrestled against the fear and the desire to quit.

Instead, I realized, I've found the limit. I'm at the end—this is far as I can go.

This sense of relief came over me because I had admitted to myself that I could not do it. I didn't have to run any more; I had tried.

While I waited for the others to realize I'd gone missing, I ate a snack. And then another. I drank some water. Pretty soon, I had eaten all my snacks and drank all my water. It got hot, and flies and mosquitoes started dive bombing me because I was a sitting target.

The only food source for ten square mile around was with my support crew. After contemplating the metaphysical implications of quitting, I realized that no one was coming to my rescue any time soon. I was hot, sun burned, hungry, thirsty, and bug-bit. I felt like a kite without the wind, useless. I knew I had to get up and get moving, but I had already quit.

This is where I entered into a dialogue with God. I prayed, "Lord, I quit. I can't do it anymore. I've gone as far as I can go." Then I remembered these words God had spoken to me, "across Mongolia in the summer of 2013." I had seen His miraculous hand at work to get us here, to get even this far.

Maybe, I reasoned, I should try that thing called faith.

But I didn't have enough faith for 1,500 miles. Didn't even have enough faith for 30 miles. In fact, I lacked the faith to even make it the 3 miles to the support vehicle.

I decided to tentatively test God in this. I asked him for the faith to take one step.

I had come to the end of my pity party, and it was only there at the end of all that when I thought, Oh, maybe I should turn to God. It was right there in the dust by the side of the road that I learned something very important: faith is not a passive thing; it's an active one.

I decided to put my new faith into action for that one step. I got my dusty bottom up off the road, turned to face the eastern horizon, and lifted my right foot to move forward.

Boom. My running shoe touched the dirt, and suddenly it was as though I heard God clap His hands one single, short time. "THAT was what I was waiting for!" I felt Him say.

God had been eagerly waiting for me to take that one step because now my faith had released His grace to operate in my life. That first step was by faith, but the next step was by grace. And so was the next and the next and the next.

By faith, through grace. Hebrews 11 talks about all kinds of different things that people have done by faith—overthrowing kingdoms, quenching flames of fire, and so much more. Tucked into this description of faith in action is a passive phrase: "received promises."[13] When you look that phrase up in the original language, the language is that of an athlete throwing the javelin and hitting the mark.

Receiving God's promises is an active thing.

When we engage our faith, it releases God's grace. One of the seminal verses in all of Scripture says, "For it is by grace you have been saved, through faith—and this is not from yourselves, it is the gift of God— not by works, so that no one can boast."[14] People typically think of this verse as it pertains to salvation, which is a terrific understanding of it.

---

13   Hebrews 11:32-35
14   Ephesians 2:8-9

But the truth is, the entire economy of the kingdom of God operates on grace, through faith.

When we step out in faith, it releases God's grace to operate in our lives. The easiest way I can describe it is that God adds His super to our natural.

As long as I stayed sitting in the dust, God would let me try to do things in my own strength and power. On my own power, I got myself about a hundred kilometers through Mongolia. I made it exactly six days, And God let me get that far.

But the moment I stepped out in faith, every step after that was grace. I started operating in faith, by grace, every day. Every morning I woke up so sore that it took about fifteen minutes for me to just stand up. But I told myself every day, "If I can stand up, I can walk. And if I can walk, I can run today—by faith, through grace."

That is literally how I got all the way across Mongolia, not on my own strength because that lasted less than a hundred miles. It was by faith, through grace. When people ask me how I did it, how I ran across Mongolia, this is how I answer.

In many ways, this is where the trip really began. The first part was just the warm-up, just enough to bring me to the end of myself. The rest of the journey was all God's grace.

INTO "ACTION"

Be assured, running in God's grace didn't mean that I no longer got tired, was sore, or got bugs in my teeth. Those were realities. However, the truth is that God had called us to run across Mongolia in the summer of 2013, and when I grabbed hold of that promise by faith, that's when God was able to do His part.

This is important: God's promises are always guaranteed, but they are not automatic.

Going back to Hebrews 11 for a moment, we read an interesting verse that says, "And by faith even Sarah, who was past childbearing age, was enabled to bear children because she considered him faithful who had made the promise."[15] Sarah received the ability to bear a child, but she had to take God's word and put it into action—literally into "action" with her ninety-nine-year-old husband. The rest is history: Isaac was born, the first of the Jewish nation.

God fulfilling his promise to Abraham was not automatic; it required action. You can sit on your rear in the dust saying all the right things ("We're just believing God") but not doing anything. And when we do this, our words actually mean we are simply waiting around to see what's going to happen.

Newsflash: nothing is going to happen until you take a step. You can sit there all day long, all year, your whole life . . . waiting. I don't care how much "faith" you claim to have, until you get up and take a step of faith, nothing is going to happen.

So what step is God waiting on you to take right now?

Take a moment right now to zero in on the greatest point of pain or need in your life. Everything else is probably within your realm of ability, and you may not need God's grace to deal with the rest of your life (foolishly—we should need Him in every area of our lives). But the point at which you are in the most pain or have the most need will show your need for His grace.

When you have honestly identified that place in your life, it's time to get into the Bible. Get your lab coat on because it's time to do some serious research. Tear into the Word and the look for promises about that point of need or pain. Our world is full of wonderful resources that make searching the Bible as easy as googling something. With a few clicks of the mouse, you can become a Bible scholar, an archaeologist

---

15   Hebrews 11:11

out to dig up the life-changing truths that will speak to your situation.

The Bible isn't just God's story, it's full of every promise that pertains to the human condition. He has given us everything we need for living a godly life.[16] God will honor every promise He has made, and I guarantee He has something to say about what you're going through. And when you find out what He has to say, you will find a promise contained in that. And when you get that promise, hold onto it—be a bull rider with that unyielding grip right before the bull is let out of the shoot; be a bulldog that simply won't let go after you get your teeth into it.

Want to know how to get across your Mongolia? Grab onto God's promises, and don't let go.

---

16   2 Peter 1:3

CHAPTER 12

CHANGE OR DIE

Hardships often prepare ordinary people for extraordinary destiny.

– C.S. Lewis

Lissa had not worried about the running at all . . . until it started. When she saw that I wasn't able to cover the necessary miles, it quickly hammered home on her detail-oriented mind that we were messing with a schedule that included booked flights and other considerations, not the least of which was that the support team wasn't cheap per day. Too much was riding on our schedule for the ease and convenience of the team to dictate things to us. The team's needs had to be subject to the needs of the expedition as a whole.

The stage was getting set for a major paradigm shift for how we were conducting the expedition. But it would require a complete change in how we conducted our daily activities. How would the team respond?

I knew that this change was important for the success of our mission, but I also knew that language and cultural barriers, not to mention the inertia of how we'd been doing things for the first few weeks, could make the change really difficult.

Would the Fellowship survive the change?

TIME FOR A CHANGE

We could not get a rhythm at first. Our early strategy was to make camp about once every two to three days and for me to travel to and from my running miles via one of the two support vehicles that accompanied us. This added hours to my day but simplified our setup and teardown. It was easy on everyone . . . except me.

And it was killing us. It was killing my ability to put on miles, and if left uncorrected, it would ruin the whole expedition.

The kind of guy I am, it was hard for me to lead in the direction that what was best for me, as the guy putting on the miles, would ultimately be best for the team. It seemed as though what was best for the team should dictate how we operated. So many considerations said it was best to camp every few days and then only pack up and move when necessary, not the least of which included the availability of water. However, the whole schedule would come apart if I could not cover the necessary miles in a day.

We tried to make it work for about three weeks, but I was paying the price. One of the critical moments of the whole trip occurred when Lissa and I, the leaders of the expedition, decided it had to change. "I can't do more miles," I said. I simply couldn't do it. Something had to change.

Our Mongolian support team didn't understand; if anything, they really liked the way we had been doing things. Only one of the drivers had to go out with me each day, so the other one got to sleep all day. We had to be firm, and it caused some tension with our fixer, Tulga, to change the very nature of our camp rhythm.

Our method of operation had me eating breakfast with everyone else before getting in one of the vehicles to drive to where I had left off running the day before. Sometimes this took hours! The driver would try to stay with me most of the day in that support vehicle. We were burning up gas at a much faster rate than we had anticipated because of this, and it added hours to my already grueling day—hours I was not really able to rest or recover but wasted each day.

So I had to make an unpopular decision, but I'll just let you in on a little secret: when you're in charge, you have to make unpopular decisions that don't always appear to be for the best.

NO WATER

The crisis issue that led to my unpopular decision began with a lack of water. In some ways, this was probably the lowest point in the trip on a bunch of different levels.

It began on a rainy day. I was tired, wet, and cold as I finished my miles. The kicker? We had no water. I had drunk all of mine on the road, and we couldn't camp where I finished my miles because there was no water nearby and we had none stored. We had no choice but to mark the spot on the GPS so we could return to it and drive on in search of water.

This isn't a problem we face in the West. How often have you ever had to go completely without water—or not know when you would be able to get it? But if you've ever had to run or hike without water, you'll understand how basic a necessity this is.

I was so tired, at this point I really didn't care. I just wanted something to drink and my sleeping bag. We piled into the support vehicles and headed down the muddy, rained-out road. Through potholes, big puddles, and over bumps, we rocked and rolled our way along as the sun began to set. When we started, we had four or five hours of sunlight left, but as we drove, the sun got lower and lower, and we saw no town, settlement, or source of water. We had no choice but to go on, even though we were all hungry and tired.

The sun went down, set, and was gone. Still, we clattered along the horrendous roads trying to find a town, lake, or river. About ten o'clock that night, we dragged into something like a truck stop, except there were no permanent building or gas pumps. A collection of tents along the roadside offered a meal and a place to park for traveling vehicles crossing the steppes. Tulga hopped out to talk to the man in charge, and he came back to report that they didn't have any water either. They had to drive about forty-five minutes up to a valley spring in order to draw water about once a week, and they had none to spare for us.

We tried to find out where it was, but the guy told us that we would never find it in the dark and that we might as well wait for morning. We set up our tents next to the gerrs beside the road and made out the best we could. Unfortunately, that meant I wouldn't be able to run the next day.

I was already dehydrated, and I wouldn't be able to run without water. It would be like trying to start a car I'd run empty the day before—it just couldn't happen. But this wasn't just an issue for me. If you think I was cranky when I got dehydrated, try having two children and six other members of the expedition all thirsty.

This was a crisis, but there was little we could do. So we unpacked in the dark and simply tried to get some sleep. We had not unpacked the cook tent to set up the kitchen, so there was no breakfast in the morning other than a few little snacks. Order of business number one: find water.

The guy in charge offered to send his eight-year-old son with us. He had a five-gallon Jerry can and a little dipper for scooping water. It was as big as he was! He hopped in our van with us, and off we clattered across the steppes to find the spring.

The good: he led us right to it. The bad: the spring was not much more than a trickle. It was just enough for his family, who drank very little water like most Mongolians, and they probably only used it to make tea.

As the sun climbed higher and higher, he used the little scooper to fill the five-gallon can one little scoop at a time. We could only watch, hungry from having missed dinner the night before and only scavenging for breakfast. It seemed like it took all day for him to fill the can, but it probably was only thirty or forty-five minutes, which doesn't seem that long, but we needed at least twenty gallons.

We gathered as much water as we could in about an hour, and by now it was past lunchtime—another missed meal. We faced a major decision, one we had not encountered before: what do we do? I couldn't run on an empty stomach and with very little water. If I didn't get in my miles, we wouldn't make it to the border on time.

Suddenly, we faced a massive moral crisis. The obvious answer was to get in the vehicles and drive ahead to another campsite, which still would be pushing it because we had to take the kid back and drop him off. But if we skipped this day because of these factors, we would be crossing a threshold. If we would bend because of this, what else would cause us to fudge? Would we skip ahead every time some little thing didn't work out?

What did our integrity demand? We had told our donors and sponsors that we would run fifteen hundred miles. Losing thirty miles of that isn't a very big percentage, but it still isn't the full fifteen hundred we promised. On the other hand, fifteen hundred miles was a made-up number, a nice round one we picked because it was approximately the distance "across Mongolia." In reality, the plan was never to run from tip to tip but from certain points on the borders.

Lissa and I had a very intense conversation about all this. I was exhausted and starving, and my goal was to help kids and get all the way across the country. She was deeply concerned about our integrity and what we would tell people, whereas I was much less concerned about what other people thought than on what was in our hearts.

Meanwhile, every minute we sat talking about it was one minute less time for action. Our water jugs were nearly full, it had been almost twenty-four hours since the team had eaten a meal, and we considered camping right there, but the mosquitoes were pretty bad.

Suddenly, the weight of it came crashing down. "I cannot keep on going, changing camp once every five days!" I said.

"What do you want to do?" Lissa asked.

"We need to move camp every day."

It just came out of my mouth. I had no idea how we would do it. I thought it would be hell on the team and my family to tear down and set up camp every day. But if we didn't, there's no way I would be able to make up the lost miles.

My wife is amazing! "Well," she said, "if that's what we need to do, we didn't just come here to camp and be comfortable and have fun. We came to accomplish the purpose, and if that's what we need to do in order to accomplish that purpose, that's what we're going to do!"

This was our wakeup call that our tactics needed to change. The success of our mission hung on how we proceeded forward.

"CHANGE" ISN'T A FOUR-LETTER WORD

Our new system had the team packing up camp daily as I set out to cover my miles. This would be harder on them, but Lissa later informed me that in some ways it was better, even for the team. Everyone had something to do every day now. Everyone had a job, everyone had something to focus on and keep their attention. The team wasn't bored anymore.

When I told Tulga what we were doing, he resisted. He liked the way we had been doing things because it was easier. It took a lot of effort to communicate to someone for whom English was a second language, but it had to happen. The drivers didn't like it, and Duya, our cook, didn't care for it either.

And I will tell you this: once the decision was made and Lissa and I presented a unified front, everyone came into line. We had to put our foot down and say, "This is how it's going to be, so get used to it." And then I went to bed.

But once the daily routine of camp had shifted for the better, it was obvious that this change needed to be made. The biggest challenge we faced was that every day when I was on about mile twenty, EK, driving the Russian van with Duya on board, had to go ahead to find a new camping spot. We tried to mark via the odometers where the camp would be, but still it could be like looking for a needle in a haystack to find the camp, which was often off the road, somewhere close to the end of my miles. I set my mind for thirty miles a day, but it ended up being pretty variable — and whenever it wasn't even close, I would get pretty upset.

Often a support vehicle would come rattling down the road to meet me. "We found a good camp," they'd say. I'd ask where it was, and they'd admit, "Well, it's another five kilometers down the road."

I would sigh and simply have to trudge on. Most of the time, I would have to walk or shuffle these last miles—I just couldn't find the energy to run them.

From the time we began this new procedure, everything went much more smoothly. We found our rhythm and daily routine, and it seemed like miles were easier somehow.

THE NEW NORMAL

Our changes to the way we camped each day meant that everybody had something to do every day, all the time. It took Lissa and the kids about half an hour to unpack our tent and stuff. They became true masters at getting camp torn down and set up every day, from sleeping bags and mattresses to the rain fly. Camping in foul weather held little challenge for us now.

It took them about half an hour to get the cook tent set up as well, and they didn't even have the same type of convenience items that we so take for granted. If we had only had a home-improvement store in Mongolia, we could have bought just a few things that would've made life a lot easier. Oh what we would have done for a wheeled plastic hub! As it was, we did things Mongolian style, which included eating off of china at every meal (and, of course, porcelain plates and cups had to be repacked carefully every day). I am sad to say that I don't think any of the cups survived the trip.

The worst and hardest days by far were when it rained when we set up camp or rained when it was time to pack up. It was utterly miserable! Everything was wet, and we had few ways of drying things out, but I'll get into that more later.

For most of the trip, the weather was in the 80s and 90s during the day, which is great for camping, and would get down into the 40s at night. However, toward the end of the trip, it was dropping below freezing at night, and we had to knock the frost off our tent every morning.

Our tent became a mobile home for us, and we had this sense that after the running was over and I was "home" for the night, this family time could just go on forever. We escaped into The Lord of the Rings every night, and the kids ended up not wanting to go home!

None of us would have traded being together for the world.

We would end our days by saying that no matter what had happened, all was well that ended well. We were together, we were careful to keep our sleeping bags dry, and our tent was a little embassy of our family on distant foreign soil. We began calling it our Fortress of Solitude.

NECESSARY DECISIONS

Forcing a change on the rest of the group that primarily benefited me was hard to do. Yet, it had to be done. Our Fellowship had balanced on the edge of a knife, and if we fell, the entire expedition could fail. If I gave in to the desire to appease other people, or if I simply was a selfish jerk, I think we wouldn't have made it much further.

But something had to give, and instead of me, it was the dysfunctional rhythm we had tried so far. The thing of it is that nothing was obviously broken; we were crossing Mongolia. But we were doing it in a way that wouldn't meet our requirements. I bet right now there are things in your life that are sort of working. You limp along from day to day because you don't necessarily know what to change or don't think that people will go along with you if you try to change it. However, if it's not working—if you're unable to fulfill the purpose God has given you or carry out His mission in your life—it's time for a change. It's time to cowboy up, take responsibility for the leadership of your life, and make what could be an unpopular choice to change your life.

So, what changes need to be made in your life? If there is anything keeping you from finding a godly/healthy rhythm? I suggest you get on your knees and pray intensely about what needs to change. Then, do it—regardless of the consequences.

The Russia-Mongolia Border
Standing on the far western border with our heavily armed border guards, Lissa covertly took this photo of the gate leading into Russia. This was my starting line.

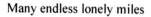

Many endless lonely miles

Brian and Tulga at breakfast. The prayer flags in the background are Bible verses and prayers written by friends back home.

Saying goodbye to our medic Jason who joined us for the first ten days. Knowing he would be back home within thirty hours of this picture when we still had months ahead of us was emotionally crushing.

Beautiful camping in an area we named "Marmot Valley." The Mongolians call marmots "prairie rats."

Kai and Selah wearing their adventure hats and standing on the edge of what Mongolians call a "settlement." The heat of the July sun was oppressive and inescapable.

Selah and Lissa sleeping in the "Goat Motel." The scent from the bed sheets smelled like yak sweat and cheap Russian cologne. Needless to say, we slept on our sleeping pads ON TOP of the sheets.

Jacob the biker—even though he only spent one night in our camp on his solo, around-the-world bike trip, we connected on a deep level because we both understood the lonely hardships of being on the road.

A quick 500-mile mark celebration on top of a mountain pass with a prayer shrine in the background.

Want a killer tan line? Follow this simple recipe: spend twelve hours a day for two-and-a-half months in the Mongolian sun; add sweat, dust, and sunscreen; don't shower . . . and voila!

Support vehicle sandwich, which made me think about sandwiches, specifically turkey sandwiches . . . I was always thinking about food.

Rest days often included endless rounds of the only board game we brought with us.

"Riding the Black Dragon" Running on pavement was the worst. The asphalt was hard on the joints, the cars were deadly, and the endless road was a merciless psychological demon taunting me with thoughts of giving up.

The heartbreaking reality of life in the city dump

Lissa and Selah distributing food to children in the Gerr district in the capital city of Ulaanbaatar.

Selah, Lissa, and Kai getting their picture with Chinggis Khaan.

Just hangin' with the boys.

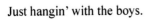

Some days the mosquitoes were so bad that bug spray seemed only like seasoning for them. Running with a cheesecloth shroud helped, but I looked like a weird runaway bride shuffling across the Mongolian steppe.

Kids love kids.

Hydrate or die.

A happy moment deep into September when we reached Choibalsan— the last settlement on the remote eastern plains before reaching the border with China.

After 27 consecutive marathons, 6 pair of running shoes, 200 pounds of peanut butter and Nutella, setting a world record for the first person to run across Mongolia, and raising over $50,000 dollars for the cause, we crossed the "finish line" at the eastern border of Mongolia where it touches China.

The Across Mongolia Expedition Team

From left to right: Duya, Selah, Azuka, Lissa, Kai, Brian, EK, Greg Wheeler, Tulga, Amra, Jeff Ryan, and Venus

CHAPTER 13

SHIVERING, STARVING, AND LOST

Tough times never last; tough people do.
– Robert H. Schuller

One time when I was in high school, my buddy Ben Marshall and I decided to climb Mount Rainier, specifically Liberty Ridge. We were two days into the climb and above 10,000 feet (which is merely a trail-head in Colorado). But for Rainier, we were way up there. The second night, a big storm blew in and pinned us down overnight with heavy snows, and by the next day, the snow was still coming down pretty heavily. We still had a lot of climbing left to do, but after sizing up the conditions, we decided that we didn't want to take any chances with avalanches. We were forced to turn around.

What had taken us three days to climb, we hiked down in a day. My buddy Ben is part robot—he just doesn't get tired. I wore myself out just trying to keep up with him as we made our way back down to the trailhead.

Once we got below the snow line, the precipitation changed from snow to rain, and it rained on us the whole rest of the way down. Our packs, already heavy with gear, got more and more heavy as they soaked up the water like giant sponges. By the time we got to the trailhead, I felt like I was one of those struggling tractors in a monster truck tractor race, dragging a sled behind me.

Back at the car, I changed into some dry clothes, and we headed for Ben's uncle's house in Seattle. On the drive, I began to shiver uncontrollably, and we ended up having to stop at a hospital in Yakima. I went into the ER with a resting heart rate of 120, still shivering uncontrollably.

Hypothermia had snuck up on me like some sort of crazy ninja assassin! I was an experienced mountaineer and pursuer of outdoor adventures, and even though I knew what to look out for, hypothermia had snuck up on me and taken me down. Warm fluids and I don't know how many sandwiches later, I felt fine, but it was not a good experience.

So, fool me once, shame on you. Fool me twice . . .

STALKED IN MONGOLIA

Fast-forward more years than I would like to admit to about two thirds of the way through the trip across Mongolia. It was just another day running . . . in the rain. Now, I know—rain. Believe me, I've done rain! This was nothing unusual, just another day in the rain. The only difference was that on this particular day, it was a little bit cooler. When the outside air temperature is over fifty degrees, even if you're wet, as long as you keep moving you're okay. If it gets much below fifty degrees, if you're not prepared, you enter an ideal hypothermia zone. (Cue the Twilight Zone™ music.)

It was August now, so we were losing light a little bit sooner than at the start of the trip, and this particular day I was finishing my miles later than usual. So it wasn't just a little cooler; it was a little later too. Because it was getting dark, I was finishing my run with my headlamp on. One of the support vehicles was a little ways behind me with the headlights on to give me more light, which was both comforting and yet tickled a survival mechanism that running five hundred miles in Mongolia had perfected—cars were the enemy! So as I ran on this chilly, wet night, I had to fight the unintended psychological pressure to hurry up and watch out for the car behind me.

I should've been in the meeting tent eating, saying, "All's well that ends well," but there I was out on the muddy road feeling that if I were just stronger, I could run faster. Part of me wished that the support vehicle wasn't there, and then I could just suffer in peace.

Somewhere along the line, I began to recognize the very first preliminary stages of hypothermia as I trudged along the road. I realized I wasn't racing the support vehicle or anyone else; I was racing that quiet assassin, hypothermia. Either I would finish my miles and get into the support vehicle, where I could get dry and warm to steer away from hypothermia, or the assassin was going to catch me before I finished my miles.

It was a race, and the stakes were high.

I couldn't just stop; I had to run. Doing what I was doing, I couldn't let small things keep me from putting in the miles—otherwise I wouldn't ever do them! I just had to push through.

The moment my GPS watch ticked thirty miles, something gave out; I just collapsed to the ground. I was totally exhausted, and I recognized not only was I soaked to the bone, my inner meter was well below "E." I wasn't just out of gas, I had entered into a negative zone.

Lissa, playing Sam to my Frodo, jumped out of the support vehicle and scooped me up, supporting me as we got back in for the drive to camp. I didn't have any dry clothes to change into, and the forty-minute drive back to camp in the wet clothes was just the opening the assassin needed.

By the time we rolled into camp, I could barely stand or walk. Everyone else had eaten. Duya had kept hot food ready for me, but I was so exhausted I had no appetite. I just wanted to crawl in my sleeping bag.

"You have to eat," Lissa told me.

"I can't," I told her. "I'm just too tired. I just want to go to bed."

She helped me into our tent, peeled off my wet clothes, got me into dry ones, and jammed me into my sleeping bag. Now that I was no longer focused on running, I was able to shift my internal diagnostic mechanism over to health-mode. I was trying to get an accurate assessment of how cold I was, how tired I was, and most importantly, how deeply the hypothermia ninja had stabbed me. I recognize that I was definitely in the early stages and needed to turn it around—fast!

Even though I had no appetite, we needed to get calories in me right away. With only my face showing from my sleeping bag, I relied on Lissa to nurse me with warm Gatorade and globs of peanut butter, which even without an appetite, I could still eat. It was soft and stuck to the roof of my mouth, and it did taste good. Together with the warm Gatorade, I could feel the calories getting down inside me and sinking into my bones.

The situation teetered on the edge. Would the calories be enough? Lissa kept nudging me awake to drink more Gatorade and swallow my peanut butter, which was still in my mouth as I drifted in and out.

Chew, Brian.

Swallow.

Repeat.

DODGING A BULLET

I woke up the next morning feeling like I had had a fitful, restless sleep. However, Lissa had fended off the assassin! The hypothermia hadn't gotten any worse, and though I was very weak, my appetite was back. I devoured breakfast, and then I rooted around for last night's leftovers. After gorging myself and making up for my losses, it was time to confront a new day.

It was dawn on the steppes. Thirty miles awaited me along the road. There was no time for sympathy, weakness, or days off to recover; it was time for another fun-filled day in Mongolia.

It would've been really nice to have a medic with us at that point in the trip, but we weren't that lucky. However, I was blessed with an amazing wife who understood the power of peanut butter and warm Gatorade. Those were our weapons of choice against the quiet assassin, but they proved to be enough. I had dodged a bullet, and I knew it. I lived to run another day.

All's well that ends well.

THE 500-MILE MARK AND PERPETUAL MOTION

In any other circumstances, running 500 miles would be a significant moment worth celebrating. Lissa and the kids were very excited when we reached the 500-mile mark, but I didn't really know if I wanted to hear their cheers because reaching the 500-mile mark only reminded me that I still had a thousand left to go.

So we stopped to take some pictures and rest for about ten minutes. I ate something, and we looked out over the road ahead. We happened to be at the top of the highest pass of the Khangai Range, a rare change in elevation where the road went through the saddle of some low mountains. The entire world seemed to stretch out below us. Miles waiting for me to run, I admit, I was in no mood to celebrate.

Eager to get back on the road, we set out. The support vehicles went on ahead, leaving me with the relatively easy task of running downhill for an extended period of time. Along the rugged road, you could see various car parts that had rattled off—drive shafts, mufflers, differentials, even wheels. The road had wound up the far side of the mountain, but down the side, even though it was relatively steep, the road was pretty much straight down the mountain. As I was running along, I even saw an old truck tire in a ditch.

A sudden thought popped into my head, I wonder how far that truck tire would roll down the mountain road if I got it going? In case you haven't noticed this about me, I am prone to these little-boy fancies— the Peter Pan in me shining out. My curiosity became insatiable, and I rationalized that having just crossed the 500-mile mark, I owed it to myself to celebrate in my own way. Not only that, this was an experiment—this was for the sake of science!

It was a big tire, probably from an eighteen-wheeler from one of the big Chinese convoy trucks. I wasted about two miles' worth of energy dragging it out of the ditch, thankful for my CrossFit™ workouts before I left for Mongolia. I got the tire positioned perfectly in the middle of the road, looked around in case there were any cars (surprise, surprise, I was the only living thing for miles), and started giggling to myself like a giddy little schoolboy. I started rolling the tire with my hands in front of me, helping pick up speed, and in no time at all, it was rolling so fast I was having trouble keeping up with it. With one last, mighty shove, I hurled it down the mountainside.

I laughed out loud, most likely an insane cackle, with a boyish smile on my face as the tire hit a slick little bump and caught big air. Faster and faster. I began to realize how much energy that big-truck tire had. If by some miracle, a car did manage to get on the road, it would be catastrophic, let alone if a yak decided to cross the road!

My mischievous science experiment turned into amazement, and then mild fear of what I had unleashed. Would it ever stop? Or would it roll all the way to the capital?

The tire started to drift toward the ditch on the downhill side of the road, skipped off a rock, and bounced really high before crashing into the bottom of a ravine. It crossed a gap of about ten yards before bouncing on the other side and began to roll uphill. Finally, it came to a stop—without tipping over! It then began to roll backwards toward a creek, and I seriously thought that, like some sort of cartoon, I had created perpetual motion, and it would never stop. It finally did though, and I admit, I was a little disappointed. But I had something fun to share that night in the meeting tent around dinner.

DOG WITH A CABLE

I have talked about dogs before, but I want to mention one in particular. While we were still west of Ulaanbaatar, we had a trio of canine visitors. Our Mongolian teammates treated dogs with deserved contempt because frequently they were wild and savage creatures. But these three were actually friendly with big woolly coats and looked like crosses between a German Shepherd and a Golden Retriever. The dogs hung out around our camp, and the kids wanted to pet them, but we had to remind them that these dogs in Mongolia are nothing like the dogs we would encounter in America, so they needed to keep their distance.

One of them walked really funny. He limped, and sort of walked sideways, and as he spent more time with us, he grew comfortable enough to let us get closer. We noticed he had a really tight leather strap around his neck, cutting deep into his fur. Attached to this leather strap around his neck was a large broken car part, like something from a transmission or differential. The heavy, rusted piece had a hunk of steel cable hanging off of it that he dragged everywhere he went. The cable was well-worn from having been dragged along the ground, and all his fur had been rubbed off where it rubbed against his neck and shoulder.

The sympathetic American in us wanted to help it. In the land of poverty and injustice, we became fixated on how to help this dog. My daughter especially cried that we had to help him.

I went to my bag and pulled out my Leatherman™ multi-tool, and I coaxed the dog to come closer. I managed to pull back his fur to expose the tight leather strap, and I carefully slipped the Leatherman's knife underneath the tight leather. As I cut through the leather, the dog winced and whimpered in pain, though I don't think I was hurting him.

The moment I cut through the strap, the car part and steel cable fell to the ground, and he yelped and ran off. I picked up the burden he had been carrying and that had rubbed him raw. Together, the car part and cable probably weighed fourteen or fifteen pounds.

A few minutes later, the dog came back. Interestingly, he still walked with the same sideways gait even though he no longer had the strap, part, or cable hanging off him. If I have ever seen a dog who looked grateful, this one did. The whole rest of the afternoon, he stayed right by my side and slept outside our tent.

We left the next day, and I watched as he walked away with a limp, sideways as though still bound. As I ran, couldn't help but think of the parallels in our lives with sin and the fact that Jesus makes us free.

LOST AND ALONE

About 500 miles into our adventure, our route led us to one of

Mongolia's rivers, the Shiver River, which is also the name of a type of pine tree. In the West, we don't think much of crossing rivers because we have these novel items called bridges. The thing is, in Mongolia, bridges are optional. Some of the flowing water in Mongolia doesn't require a bridge even though some are full-fledged rivers that can't be crossed.

Industrious Mongolians have built bridges of logs and river stone, and while some are passable, most are pretty rickety and decrepit. For us, that meant a forty-kilometer detour to the north to the closest concrete bridge (which we learned about by talking to the locals) and would require a forty-kilometer drive to get back to our route once we were on the other side of the river.

Being the bright guy that I am, and a hopeless optimist, I suggested, "Why don't I cross this bridge, and I'll continue running down the road. You guys cross up at the concrete bridge, and come back for me. It should only take a few hours, right? You can catch up with me down the road." The funny thing is, no one who knew better corrected me.

After lunch, we decided it was an acceptable risk, so after being resupplied with food and water and hugs and kisses, I made my way across the rickety bridge that would support older vehicles and resumed running my miles. We had devised a "trail of breadcrumbs" system before we even left for Mongolia, so any time I reached a fork in the road, I would leave the piece of bright orange surveyors tape to indicate my direction.

That sounded pretty reasonable in our living room in Oklahoma, and even still as I loaded up with surveyors tape and headed out. But what I discovered is that in Mongolia, there's a big margin for error. Namely, there are so many forks in the road that I ran out of tape really quickly. And many of the two-track roads blended together, so I could have simply run tape everywhere.

Out of tape after crossing that rickety bridge, I had to decide whether or not to go on. My Western desire for productivity conflicted directly with the circumstance, so I made the only logical choice—plunge on into the unknown and leave a sporadic trail of granola-bar wrappers turned shiny-side out.

Five hours later, there was no sign of the support vehicles. I was out of granola bar wrappers, even though I had torn them in half. Making matters worse, as I paralleled a small lake, I could see a road in the distance peppered with occasional traffic.

I had a horrible, sick feeling that maybe I had gotten off on the wrong road somewhere in one of those many branches. From two miles away, there would be no way for the support vehicle to see me where I was. Yes, I had a radio, but the battery was starting to go out. I was maybe six hours out at this point.

Compelled to go on, I kept thinking that if I could get over the next little micro-rise in the relatively flat countryside, I would have a vantage point. But every time I crested a little rise, I would see one a few miles ahead and think that if I could get to that one, I would be able to see better.

The sick, sinking feeling got worse as I noticed that it was probably now just half an hour before sundown. I kept going, past the lake, and mercifully I arrived at a spot where the road I had noticed before merged back into the one I was on. Exhausted, out of water, out of food, with the sun going down and my radio batteries dying, I knew I was in a bad spot.

Every thirty seconds, I tried sending a call on the radio, and as the sun kissed the horizon, I noticed that my radio was no longer transmitting. It just beeped at me. The sun started to melt behind the horizon, and as the shadows grew, I turned my little red blinking safety light on that I had clipped to my vest.

With every minute, the odds of the crew being able to find me were getting worse. Alone on the Mongolian steppes, with night coming on, I would be very difficult to spot, and it would be impossible to see my trail markers, if they could have seen them at all even in good light. Worse yet, the desert-like Mongolian climate meant that during the day it was boiling hot and I ran in a t-shirt and shorts, but with night came desert cooling and temperatures in the forties.

Off toward the lake, I could still make out dust from vehicles occasionally, but I was afraid that if I left the road to head toward that, it would make finding me even harder for the team. Five to eight miles in the distance around the lake, I could see the lights of some tourist camp, but I wasn't even sure I could make it, as I'd done more than a marathon that day already.

With the sun nothing but a faint glow on the horizon, I suddenly heard something musical: "Bria—." It wasn't even my full name I heard before my radio cut out, but I knew that if I had heard anything, it meant the team was close, within three kilometers. Then, blessedly, I saw lights on the same road I was on and recognized the distinct blue of Venus' Lexus HID headlights.

As they pulled up, I nearly collapsed with relief. Everyone had been stressing out, fearing for me, and looking for me. The kids exploded onto me with hugs, and Tulga was visibly shaken by nearly losing me.

"We thought we'd lost you!" Lissa said breathlessly, clamping me in a hug I just melted into.

In the search for me, they hadn't had time to set up camp, so we headed down to the lake area where the tourist camp was set up. They had gerrs set up with floors and even beds; it was like the nomadic equivalent of a hotel! We spent the first night in weeks in an actual bed, and I just collapsed and slept.

In the aftermath of the nearly-tragic river crossing and Brian-losing experience, I learned that the "quick 40K" the locals had indicated turned out to take much longer because the roads were so bad. It took them six hours to get up to the bridge, back, and find me. As was my habit, I said, "Once again, we have cheated death and lived to tell the tale." Another favorite cliché came up as well, which we said over and over again after encounters with horrible mosquitos, running out of water, miserable nights, or getting lost on bad roads: "All is well that ends well."

CHAPTER 14

WORRY'S NOT WORTH IT

A small body of determined spirits fired with unquenchable faith in their mission can alter the course of history.

— Gandhi

Lissa and I both expected God to really speak to us during the trip. She brought her guitar in hopes that God would download some new songs into her spirit—*Mongolia Unplugged*, the worship album. Instead, it was work from the moment we got there to the moment we boarded the plane to leave for the States. Every moment there was something to do, and we had to be planning many steps ahead for things as basic as water.

For me, I expected that all the lonely miles I covered every day would provide the perfect canvas for God to work on. I had expected choirs of angels to be singing for us when we arrived, a high-speed connection to heaven to link up with us because we were fulfilling God's will, and for a new spiritual manifesto to take shape in my heart.

"Lord, here we are, doing Your will!" we said when we arrived, and then we waited for the heavens to open . . .

But instead of choirs of angels, I felt like I simply heard, "The instructor is always quiet during the exam." God had miraculously orchestrated so many things to even get us to Mongolia; now wasn't the time for sentiment and fluffy clouds in rainbows. It was time for us to work.

We prayed together every day—before I left, after I finished running for the day, and before every major decision. But there was no time for Lissa's worship album or for my spiritual revelations. Day after day and week after week, I would pray for Him to zap me with understanding, but no angels with manna came to minister to me by the roadside.

Instead, we clung to the promises we had already received—that we were to run across Mongolia in the summer of 2013 and a powerful scripture that really took on special meaning. Isaiah 40:31 says, "But those who wait on the Lord shall renew their strength; They shall mount up with wings like eagles, They shall run and not be weary, They shall walk and not faint." Let me tell you, when you are running across Mongolia, you meditate on this verse in a new and powerful way. There's something special about the utter and total dependence on God to accomplish the basics of your day—to simply get through.

In a way, I felt like God was saying that He had already spoken. I already had His word for me—run. He would take care of the rest.

For Lissa, it was a different challenge. In essence, we were on two different trips. I had tons of time and no one around, but she had constant demands and plenty of opportunities to grow in patience and long-suffering.

She felt that Tulga was always going past the daily running mileage and saying, "What does it matter? He has to cover the whole country anyway." He didn't understand that it mattered a great deal if I had to put on an extra couple miles at the end of a long, grueling day. He and Lissa would clash, and because she was a woman, she had a great deal of difficulty dealing with him as a co-leader of the expedition.

This came to a head the day Jason and I got lost.

"LOST" WITH JASON

One day, Jason decided to run with me for a time. The road was pretty straightforward, there were no crossroads, traffic, people, or anything really. Tulga and the rest of the crew headed out to set up camp with the promise that they would come back and get us.

It was a hot day, with a lot of mosquitoes, but if we were moving, they didn't bother us as much. Jason and I hopped out of the support vehicle and started trotting down the road into the dust left by the support vehicles. In a short time, the sound and clatter of them driving off down the road was gone, and Jason and I were left alone in the middle of nowhere.

What Jason and I couldn't know was that the rest of the team had to go a lot farther than they anticipated to find a good camping spot. This meant that it would take a lot longer to come back for us, and that would prove pivotal.

At the crawling, creeping pace of a jog, eating miles one step after another, time loses a lot of meaning. An hour crawled by, followed by another. After the first hour and a half, I started really looking for the support vehicle to come back for us, but that didn't happen. Another hour, no support vehicle. By then Jason and I were getting pretty worried, and we started discussing what could've happened. Did they miss us? Did something go wrong? Did we miss something?

The more fear distracted us, the more time seemed to slow down. The hot sun and the running drained us, and Jason ran out of water. He was also getting sunburned, and the two of us had stopped running, reduced to a walk in the Mongolian summer heat.

We had a radio for communicating with the support crew, but they were out of range, so we just continued walking down the dirt road. You start to think about a lot of things when you feel lost in the wastelands of Mongolia, and fear can be a constant companion.

By the time we saw dust on the horizon, we were completely spent. The most we had gone between visits with the support vehicle at this point was five miles, and by this point we had covered more than thirteen miles. When we're alone in the Mongolian steppes with no additional supplies than what we're carrying on our back, no access to water, and no idea where our support is, that's a world of difference.

The dust got closer, and Jason and I were praying that it was our team. Sure enough, our support vehicle came hauling up, and the drivers cheerfully said, "Hey guys! We've got a great camp set up."

Turns out, nothing was wrong. No one had died, no series of catastrophic tire blowouts had stranded the entire expedition, and grassland pirates hadn't carried off the women and children. It had just taken a little while to find and set up camp.

As Jason and I dragged ourselves into the vehicle and started zipping down the road at a pace that a jogger's mind can't really fathom after thirteen miles, I started to hydrate and reflect on the impact of fear. How often are the things we fear nothing more than relatively minor inconveniences that get blown all out of proportion by our circumstances or perspective? How often do the things we fear fail to come to pass?

For the crew, it felt like they had been gone from us about thirty minutes; for Jason and I, it felt like three days. In reality, it was a little more than three hours. Perspective means everything.

Now, we were not really "lost," though we felt like we'd been abandoned, left for dead. In a matter of a few hours, we went from a secure relationship with our support team to feeling like they'd left us to die out there. The perspective of a runner versus someone in a car makes a difference, but fear weaponizes those feelings and lack of perspective to create something that can halt us in our tracks.

A sudden onset of fear almost resulted in the premature death of our expedition, but let's just focus for a moment on the role perspective plays. The same way time flowed differently for those in a vehicle versus for two guys running, things can look very different depending on where we sit (or run, as the case may be). It's a little like the difference between expecting our food to be done when cooked in a microwave versus a crockpot—there's just no comparison. Both perspectives are good for something. We can expect our popcorn to be done in microwave time, but we wouldn't want to cook our roast, potatoes, onions, and carrots in a microwave and expect a tender, delicious meal. If we want tender and succulent, it's about the crockpot, and with that comes a wait—one that's worth it when Lissa is cooking.

So I want to propose this: the difference between the experience Jason and I had, where we were freaking out, and the experience the team had where they felt like nothing had gone wrong, was one of perspective. What perspective do you have on your problems? Are you expecting instant solutions? Do you feel like you're on the long road, alone and without support?

Take a few moments, and examine your problems with your perspective in mind. What if you could zoom out for a moment and view your challenges from God's perspective? Have you ever worried about something that turned out to be nothing at all? Of course you have. We all have had that happen to us. What if you tried viewing your problem from the view point of one year in the future? Big problems today shrink in size rapidly when we view them from an eternal perspective. Worry just isn't worth it.

MADDENING MOSQUITOS

Finding our tents a great nesting place for spiders would assuredly not be the first or last time we had trouble of the multi-legged variety. However, spiders actually weren't the worst pest we faced. On July 24th, I set out running into what I would describe as a wall of buzzing mosquitoes. Now, the mountains of Colorado and Wyoming can be pretty thick with mosquitoes in the summer. I've been in the Canadian Rockies just south of Alaska when you can't even be outside unless you want to be bled dry in a matter of moments, but what I encountered in Mongolia was by far the worst I had ever seen.

For one thing, I was in shorts and a t-shirt in order to run, so I had no protection. I couldn't put on my extra layers because it was too hot, and I didn't want to die of heat stroke in the middle of Western Mongolia with its daytime high in the upper 90s and no shade (ever). Second, some bizarre notion made us think we wouldn't need bug spray, and even if we had it, I probably wouldn't want to cover myself in those chemicals when I needed to be able to sweat to cool off.

I felt really badly for my family. In the support vehicle, they either had to have the windows rolled up, which got really hot or the windows down, letting mosquitoes inside to eat them alive. I got myself into this mess, so it was one thing for me to be eaten. I didn't worry about the team; they were getting paid to be here. But my innocent family weighed heavily on my mind.

Previously, if you were moving, the bugs weren't too bad, but that was not the case here. Helicopter-sized mosquitoes could move faster than I could. I remember running down into a low spot, a dried out, seasonal marshy area, and apparently the breeding ground for the global population of mosquitoes. They covered my face, getting in my nose and ears and mouth. If I closed my eyes, they got in my eyelashes. I was trying to run and swipe every part of my body simultaneously, and I ended up doing more swatting than running.

I got on the radio and called the support vehicle. "You've got to get me out of here!" I yelled. It was like I was trapped—they were inescapable!

"It's not that bad. Can't you just keep moving?" Tulga answered.

"No!"

Like a scene from a spy movie, the support vehicle zoomed in and opened the door so I could jump in almost mid-stride. I could almost hear the *Mission Impossible* theme. As the vehicle sped away, everyone went crazy inside trying to swat all the mosquitoes that had swarmed in after me. Flooding into the vehicle, they made one last desperate attempt to secure all the blood they needed for that season with one kill, like a thousand little wolves trying to bleed a moose to death one prick at a time.

"Guys," I said, "I can't run in this. You've got to take me to the other side of this lowland area, and then I'll hop out again." A few moments later, I was out of the truck and trotting along, leaving the mosquito trap of death behind me. I looked like some kind of chickenpox horror story from the mosquito bites all over my legs and arms, my neck, and face. But with as hard as life was at that point, this, too, I just took in stride. You got some mosquito bites? So what! Boo-hoo!

DON'T FEAR THE RUMOR RIVER

The same day I ran the mosquito gauntlet, we knew we had to make a decision about an upcoming river crossing. Tulga and I looked over the map every morning in the meeting tent where all we ate breakfast and planned out the day's route. We knew that we were coming up to a river, and Tulga got reports from locals that the bridge was out, so we would be unable to cross. The water was too high, and we might have to wait days for it to go down before we could get across. Or, we could make a one-hundred kilometer detour to the north, cross, and then come back down to pick up our road.

I certainly didn't want to run the extra miles, and we had to make the choice of whether to play it conservatively and go around, or take our chances that the water had gone down in the river enough to cross it. After weighing our options, I, the fearless leader of the expedition, made the decision: let's risk it! (Surprised?)

I had a strange peace within me that it would work out, but really I did not want to stress over a river we potentially could not cross until we were literally in front of it and discovered that we could cross it. Making decisions on *what ifs* and hearsay didn't sound like the way to go. It actually sounded more like fear than prudence.

So as I was finishing my miles on the day of maddening mosquitoes, I ran to the edge of the actual river. A collection of big trucks, Land Cruisers, and motorcycles were parked on both sides of the river, and all the drivers and passengers were out milling around. The thing was this was not the Mississippi River; it was more of a swollen, wide, braided series of creeks all running together (much like Mongolia's roads).

Our drivers didn't waste a minute and stripped down to their underwear to go give themselves a quick bath in the stream, something none of us had enjoyed in several weeks! The kids hopped out and ran to the edge of the water, where it wasn't moving too fast and splashed while swatting mosquitoes.

I was still in observation mode, too tired to go round and splash from running my miles, and so I had a great view as a young man in his twenties rode up on a little Chinese motorcycle. A girl about the same age sat behind him, and I watched as they chatted it over and he moved the motorcycle near the water. He revved it up, popped it in gear, and just launched out into the water. No one else was crossing, not even the big trucks, but these kids on a motorcycle just pulled their feet up a la Kermit the Frog(tm), his feet on the handlebars and hers wrapped around him. They bounced and skipped around, almost spun out, and nearly flooded the bike a few times, but he just kept it floored. Water shot up in a rooster tail behind them, the bike sputtered, gurgled, and steamed, and they made it across the river.

They hopped off the bike, looked it over, and the guy pulled out a rag to wipe it off before they both got back on and headed off down the road. I looked over at our drivers, who had put their buckets down and had stopped their bath midway through, to watch the spectacle. A collective shout went up from the gathered onlookers, but I was more than an entertained spectator.

I walked up to Tulga with our answer. "If that guy can do it, so can we. Let's do it." Tulga wasn't convinced, but I offered to demonstrate by walking across it. So I walked across the fast-moving, braided creek. The water was cold and wonderfully refreshing, and while the water was quick, I was able to walk in to about mid-thigh without trouble. My point proved, the crew saddled up, and we forded across as the onlookers watched.

I tell you this story for a couple of reasons. The first is that it's a fun story, especially watching the kids on the motorcycle getting across. Second, we've talked about fear and worry a bit in this chapter, and I wanted to show that the worry leading up to this river crossing was nowhere near worth the concern we'd given it. It ended up being no big deal—and an unexpected bonus, a bath!

If we had detoured around, listening to the rumor of fear and letting our worries dictate our reality, we assuredly would have lost a lot of time and covered a lot of extra ground. That false evidence appeared real, but it was only a *perception*—the perception locals had of how bad the river was. The *truth* was another matter entirely, but we did not know the truth until we were right before the obstacle.

When you step out to take on your Mongolia, I guarantee you will be confronted with false evidence that appears real and that will cause you fear and worry. Now, prudence is an important part of life (though not one I'm best known for). But wisdom dictates prudence, and fears dictate worry. The trick is knowing the difference.

I urge you to confront your fears with reality. Don't call the river impassible until you find out the truth. Don't let fear dictate your reality (which is what would have happened had we taken the detour—the reality would have been that we lost time). Instead, pay attention to the peace God gives you in your heart and ask for wisdom.

Do you know that wisdom is something God gives freely? The Bible promises, "If you need wisdom, ask our generous God, and he will give it to you. He will not rebuke you for asking."[17] Tomorrow has worries enough for itself, so instead, ask for wisdom and walk forward in faith, one step at a time.

---

17   James 1:5 NLT

CHAPTER 15

CHILLING AT THE GOAT MOTEL

Effort only fully releases its reward after a person refuses to quit.
– Napoleon Hill

If running in clouds of mosquitoes is difficult, camping in the cloud is worse. Following our river crossing, we found that there was no way to camp at the end of my miles because of the mosquitoes. About fifteen kilometers away, there was a town, so even though it was late in the afternoon, we decided to head for the town in hopes of staying in a hotel. The plan was that we would backtrack to where we had left off running, so we piled in the support vehicles and headed off down the road.

Lissa and I discussed whether or not this was a compromise, but being flexible on this outing instead of rigid would mean the success or failure of the expedition. While the ideal is to run every mile in a linear fashion, the reality was that the point was to run "across Mongolia," and I was content with simply getting the miles in, however we got them, even if that meant a little backtracking.

The purpose of this whole venture was to first obey God, and to raise money for orphans, but this perspective brought up ideological differences within the group. I didn't feel that the location of our campsite had anything to do with our integrity; we never claimed that we would "camp" our way across Mongolia. With all the detours we'd been forced to take, I was confident that any miles we were unable to run because of conditions, we would make up elsewhere.

On top of being in a low-end mosquito hatchery, as we headed off for the town, we could see a storm coming in. We had had slight rains, but nothing like this storm. It ended up being so bad, that the roads began to disappear. Because the terrain was so flat, when the rain fell in such torrents, it had nowhere to go. There was no runoff; it just collected in pools. Within five minutes, the road began to disappear under collecting pools of torrential rain.

We watched the windshield of the Cold War-era Russian van, whose windshield wipers collided with each other every fourth or fifth wipe. The road was indiscernible before us, vanishing beneath a rising lake of water. Slogging through the rising water on little more than GPS guidance, we made more impromptu stream crossings and miraculously found our way to this little town. Had we known what we were in for, we might have chosen to camp out in the flood.

GOAT MOTEL

We never called this little town by its real name; it was, and forever shall be, known only as the Goat Motel. First of all, it wasn't really a town; it was a settlement along a dirt road, with several buildings and fenced-in properties where people could set up their tents in the shadow of some old, rundown, Soviet-era government buildings. During the summer, the town is nearly completely abandoned as the residents graze their livestock out in the countryside.

Tulga went to several collections of gerr tents looking for somewhere for us to stay. Throw out any ideas you may have of what the hotel would look like because whatever they are, they don't apply. We were in Mongolia, so there were no Hiltons™, Holiday Inn Expresses™, or even a Motel 6™. A Motel 6 in Mongolia would be five-star luxury accommodations! These were more like guest rooms to rent, and I imagined that they were much like accommodations during Bible times—a little tent to rent behind a person's house or business. The one concession to modern conveniences was that they had propane tanks and stoves, which was an incredible improvement over cooking your food with dried yak dung. (The thing about cooking with yak dung is that you don't have to use flavorings. Not only does it give your food a distinctive flavor, it also gives the kitchen and eating area the same unique smell as well.)

Tulga came back saying that he had found something that he thought would work. But I know my wife: she will camp her way through Mongolia in tents and sleeping bags wherever the trail may take us, but when it comes to guest accommodations and somebody else's bed, I knew I needed to check out the accommodations first. So he and I went to see the room, and a guy opened a steel door that looked like it belonged on a prison cell. As the squeaky hinges revealed the room, I could see two beds on a dirt floor that had some sort of linoleum loosely rolled over rocks and roots. Each bed looked like some sort of nightmare Disney theme, like a twisted Russian interpretation of Mickey Mouse and Donald Duck, complete with themed sheets that have probably not been laundered since they were made and now had permanent brown stains on them. Best of all, the whole room smelled like goats had been giving birth in there.

But what was option B? Sleep out in the torrential, apocalyptic rainstorm on the flooded-out road? Beneath the dark clouds, it was hard to tell, but the sun was going down. We didn't have a lot of choices.

As evidence of how tired she was, Lissa saw the room and simply said, "Okay." So we spent the night in the Goat Motel on top of the sheets, except for my son Kai, who was so tired he just crawled beneath the sheets, put his head on the nasty pillow, and went right to sleep! The rest of us made a face like he had just stepped in something the dog left behind in the backyard and set up our sleeping pads and bags. We shared a room with Duya, the cook; the rest of the crew shared another room.

It was a rough night, and we simply wanted to get out of there as soon as possible. We intended to pack up and head back to where I had stopped running the day before, but as we got ready to leave the Goat Motel, we saw that the rainstorm had washed out the road. It would be impossible for us to go back and cover those particular miles. We would have to make them up somewhere else down the road.

According to the GPS, we had lost thirteen kilometers. We had hundreds upon hundreds yet to go, and at the moment, that small sum didn't seem to be much of an issue. However, an ideological storm was brewing within our hearts.

JASON LEAVES

Jason represented safety and familiarity to us, but his presence as another American in the group was different for Lissa. Whereas I was alone for most of the day, she was with the team all day, and language barriers and cultural differences were just the beginning of the challenges she faced daily.

The worst injury I suffered was a blister on day two or three (which persisted for maybe ten days because I couldn't stop running to let it heal), so we really didn't have much opportunity to use Jason's medical services before he left. That didn't keep us from wondering what would happen if something went wrong when he was not there.

The day Jason headed home was probably the most bleak our campsite looked—at least to those of us who remained. Jason tried, but it was obvious that he was eager to get home to his family.

For Lissa, his departure hit her less on a medical level and more on a friend level—an adult American to talk to on a daily basis was a great asset. She was losing a friend.

Worse, when Jason got in one of the support vehicles and drove off, a strange realization hit us: it was just that easy to leave. Ending our quest was only the matter of a ride to the airport. Jason would be back among his family and friends in a matter of hours, but we still had the vast majority of our trip in front of us. A homesick ache welled up inside of us.

The emotional separation with Jason had begun days earlier, a sort of natural drawing away as the Fellowship came closer to a planned fracture. Then we were hugging, saying our goodbyes, and asking Jason to tell our friends and family back home that we loved them and were doing well. We snapped one final picture, and then the next moment he was in one of the support vehicles driving across the desert, on his way home.

It was like a family member was leaving us and not coming back, and though it may sound strange, in a way it was almost like he had to "die" in my head for me to move on. As soon as his vehicle disappeared over the horizon in a cloud of dust, I knew I needed to move on. All the emotion needed to wait.

I clapped my hands and said, "Okay, he's gone. We've got stuff to do!" We got busy boiling water, airing out gear, route planning, tent repair, Mongolian bag laundry, treating sunburn, trying to catch up on hydration, and all the rest. There was always something to do.

Before he left, Jason gave a hurried crash course in the use of the suitcase full of medicines and medical equipment that he left with us. Lissa filmed everything on her phone as Jason administered an IV of intravenous fluids to me. Our medical security blanket was leaving, giving us only a hurried CliffsNotes™ version of how to care for ourselves medically. We wouldn't have any medical support until the day before we reached the capital.

Perhaps illustrating our emotional dysfunction, when the opportunity to meet two Mongolian herdsman on a motorcycle came up, we seized it as a chance to purge (in a good way) thoughts of Jason and heading for home by emptying the medical gear out of his suitcase and giving it to the cowboys. It was fun to watch them reaching into their traditional Mongolian jacket, called a *dell*, and fill this case with what they had stuffed in their coats. (It was interesting to see what they carried with them: half a bottle of cheap Russian vodka, medals that they had earned for horse riding at a festival, little bits of food like dried curd, lengths of rope, and other knickknacks that no good Mongolian herdsmen would be without.) It reminded me of an old children's cartoon character, Captain Caveman™, who could pull whatever he needed out of his beard.

The real tragedy was that Jason had hairy hobbit feet, which we had teased him about mercilessly. But it just serves to drive home the idea that the Fellowship was breaking up and the ring bearer had to go on with the quest and all the hundreds of miles yet to run.

For just a moment, Lissa broke down and cried after Jason left. Not so much for sadness of Jason leaving, although he would be missed, but more for other reasons. He was going home, and we were far from the safety and comfort of home. She cried, too, because a piece of her felt cheated. He just got to escape the misery and toil of expedition life, and that wasn't fair because we still had *so far* to go.

But the physical loss of Jason was traumatic because in some ways, it's like he died to us. So some of her tears were in mourning for losing him. It was also a good excuse to open a pressure-relief valve, a way to release days and days of built-up stress and anxiety.

"I feel completely unprepared for this," Lissa said to me as Jason left. But I remember thinking it wasn't a problem because we hadn't been ready for any of it, but so far that hadn't stopped us.

WHAT WE HAVE HERE IS A FAILURE TO COMMUNICATE

Making things interesting in daily life traveling across Mongolia was the fact that not all of our crew spoke English, at least not very well. Tulga, our fixer, spoke pretty good English, as did our driver Venus. Still, there was just so much that couldn't translate, and some of it was quite important.

Lissa had trouble in camp communicating for two reasons. First, she was a woman, and second, the language barrier. She tried to convey that some things were nonnegotiable—extremely vital and important due to our operation.

The most critical example of this was in picking the location of a campsite and sending a vehicle out to pick me up from the road every evening. The last five miles were the most dangerous part of every day, because those were the miles in between the last check-in we physically had with the crew and when they set up camp. A support vehicle would race ahead from me to meet up with the rest of the crew, and they would pick a campsite for the night. Typically this would be off the road a bit, and it was further dictated by the availability of fresh water and a host of other concerns.

Meanwhile, I was completely alone out on the road. Ideally this system resulted in me arriving at a fully set-up camp, at which point I could shovel hot food in my face and collapse into my tent. But I probably don't need to tell you that we do not live in an ideal world.

On many occasions where we had to camp away from the road, Lissa would be on high alert to make sure I found it. Armed with bright orange surveyors tape, she would try to mark the "road" (remember, the main artery across Mongolia is a hodgepodge of different dirt tracks paralleling one another), so that I would be able to follow the same course the support vehicles took. Even so, about half the time they evaded me.

The sun would be going down, and I would be looking for camp. Exhausted and at the end of my supplies of water and snacks, I counted off the last few miles of every day like a school kid watching the clock as the final few minutes of school ticked away. Lissa really was watching the clock, nervously noting how low the sun was getting and eagerly watching for me to arrive.

If it were getting late, she would tell the driver to head back and follow me so that I could find the camp. The conversation would go something like this:

Lissa: "It's getting dark. Turn right around, and go find Brian. Do you understand?"

Driver: "Yes, I go find Brian."

Lissa: "Okay, thanks."

She would begin setting up the tent and would go inside to inflate the air mattresses and ready the sleeping bags, only to come out again and find that the driver was still there. At times, it was pitch dark by then, and she would ask, "Where is Brian? Did you already get him?"

"No, I no go yet."

This is where Lissa learned patience and long-suffering—and I learned survival skills! The trouble is no one would know if I had already run right past our campsite. Which way should the driver go? East or west? In the pitch dark, finding little unlit me in the vastness of the Mongolian plains among the selection of two-lane tracks would be extremely difficult.

"What part of 'go find Brian' didn't you understand?" she wanted to scream. Often, the driver would actually get in his vehicle and head out, but only just far enough to get to the cook tent where he would stop and talk.

When a vehicle did finally find me, which was always an adventure, I would rant, "Where were you?" But seemingly no amount of attempts to communicate how important it was to follow Lissa's instructions got through to them.

Communication hiccups are pretty common to human nature. You may not have difficulty communicating with your expedition support crew, but I have yet to meet the husband and wife who don't have their own communication peccadillo. She can talk and talk about something, and he just doesn't get it. He wonders why she doesn't understand something else (which he may or may not have verbalized).

Often, our communication deficiencies can also push one another's buttons. When your deficiency matches up with an emotional bruise in your spouse (they often have the perfect match for your own wounds), the results are what we call the dance. He says this, so she says that; she says something that hits him just right, and his response triggers something back in her. Pretty soon, something relatively small can take on a life of its own, far out of proportion to the original offense.

The solution for this isn't much different than what we had to do on the steppes of Mongolia—pray for grace, and grow in patience and long-suffering. Some friends of ours find it helpful to say, "Stop the music," when one realizes that the argument they are having is part of the dance.

When you picked up this book, I bet you didn't think it would be so helpful. Marriage advice and how to handle an international-expedition team's communication issues, all in one handy volume.

THE KIDS

I mentioned earlier that we took some flak for bringing our kids with us to Mongolia. However, to us there was no other way to do it! In fact, I think they were at a great age for such an awesome adventure. Like members of the Fellowship of the Ring—hobbits to be sure!— they accompanied us on an epic quest.

We brought some schoolbooks along, and while we had a few games on my phone and our son Kai had a handheld gaming device, the kids were under strict rules about when they could use them. This wasn't simply a vacation; everyone had work to do and had to pull their own weight. The kids earned media time by getting pages of their summer schoolbooks done, so most of the time I didn't even need to ask them to do their school work; they just hopped in the vehicle to get moving that day and got started.

The first part was hard for them because we had no rhythm, and we have found that kids work best when they know what's coming and have a schedule. After the first few weeks, they had responsibilities to do every morning: packing up their stuff, getting it outside the tent, and helping if Lissa asked. If it were nice outside, when they were done with their chores, they were off like a shot.

Lissa kept things interesting by playing little games with them, like "Where will daddy turn up this time?" They would try to guess what mile they would catch up to me on. Particularly fun for me was that every night we had family time in the dubious privacy of our tent. I especially loved reading the *Fellowship of the Ring* together because I definitely felt like Lissa and I were like Frodo and Sam on a journey that was assuredly too big for us hobbits.

Typically, my family caught up to me around about the time I was on my tenth mile, and generally they got out to stretch when they caught up to me. They would then get back in the car and go another five miles, where they would set up to meet me for lunch. Lunch was one of my favorite parts of the day since I got to see my family, and I could I sneak a little cat nap while Lissa and the kids played.

But our favorite game was Rock Bottle. Empty vodka bottles litter the roads of Mongolia like wildflowers on the roadside. I mean, it's bad! The thought of how many intoxicated Mongolians are canon-balling their way across the dirt roads of their country is scary. However, they provided great target practice for us, and my son, especially, developed quite an arm. He could throw a rock at a bottle and hit it with more accuracy than anybody on the team.

Discipline wasn't a problem because Lissa came up with a pretty good method. If you have ever said, "Do you want me to pull this car over?" to your kids when they were misbehaving in the back, you already have a good idea of what she did. Binoculars in hand, she would pick a landmark in the distance (there often wasn't much to choose from), and rain or shine, Selah and Kai would have to hold hands and walk out to it and back together. It would take them a good twenty minutes I'm told. And if Lissa saw them let go even once, they would have to go back. Now you might think that this would be a great way to have sullen, resentful kids, but it had the exact opposite effect. They would come back singing and skipping.

Typically the family would check up on me one more time during the day, and then I didn't see them again until I came in at the end of the day looking for the campsite. We would be together, and everyone looked forward to mealtimes. Our cook, Duya, did a terrific job, and we would all talk. We had many wonderful conversations in the meeting tent, but they always seemed to somehow revolve around three topics: food we wished we had, how crazy the weather and roads were, and how far we still had go. About dark, like a good agrarian family, we would head to our tent for snuggling and reading time together. It wasn't long until it was time for lights out. Rinse and repeat—the same thing over and over, like *Groundhog Day* on the Mongolian steppes.

People told us it was crazy to bring our kids; I say it would've been crazy *not* to. We have never before had such a time of family bonding as we did on our trip across Mongolia. We grew closer together as a family, and the kids had a chance to see us demonstrating obedience to God in real-life, full, gritty color.

Living it out in front of our kids would often get me thinking about what we call *discipleship* in the Christian community. Jesus recruited twelve disciples, and they spent about three years marinating in His presence. The Jewish concept of discipleship means going through a particular program that consists of walking under the teaching of a Rabbi, seeing how he lived, and letting his philosophy rub off on another generation.

Discipleship doesn't happen through books or videos or just telling someone what to do. Discipleship isn't taught; it's caught. It's daily, it's real life, and it's full of the real bumps and bruises of life. Lissa and I had a chance to back up what we said with what we did in front of our children with all the filters taken away. In one room, in one car, in one place day after day, there was no separation. Everything was transparent and eminently visible to our children. For better or worse, they saw our highlights and our lowlights, and there was no disguising it. We couldn't hide behind our mask of being "perfect parents" We had to live it all out right in front of them.

I believe that one day they will look back on this experience and see not only how it brought us together as a family but how it demonstrated the reality of what we were willing to do to obey God. If discipleship is done right, the people you are discipling won't even call it that—they'll just call it living life together. So instead of preaching *at* our kids, we do life *with* them, and we trust that God shining through us makes some sort of imprint on their lives.

The biggest change I've noticed in them after our great adventure is that they love and look forward to family time. Whether it's taking a hike, going for a bike ride, or snuggling under the blankets to watch a movie, I get the sense from them that when the four of us are all together for a common objective, they feel at home, natural, and complete.

There's no way I *wouldn't* have brought my children to Mongolia!

CHAPTER 16

MANDATORY FUN

---

*Every morning in Africa, a gazelle wakes up. It knows it must move
faster than the lion, or it will not survive. Every morning a lion
wakes up and it knows it must move faster than the slowest gazelle or
it will starve. It doesn't matter if you are the lion or the gazelle, when
the sun comes up, you better be moving.*

– Maurice Greene

After the deluge that drove us into the Goat Hotel, there was a foot
or more of standing water as far as the eye could see. It turned our area
into a lake. Jesus hasn't brought me along to the water-walking stage
of my faith, so we just had to wait for the water to go down.

Also, that wasn't the first or last time we had a lot of rain. While
that storm created its own difficulty, a persistent system that seemed
to stick with us as I ran caused a whole different set of difficulties. At

one point, we slogged through nine-straight days of rain.

Now, safe and dry in our homes in America, we don't appreciate what nine-straight days of rain really means unless we are in a flood-prone area. The closest you can come to appreciating it would be if you have gone camping and been rained on for days and days.

The nine-straight days of rain luckily found us on different ground than the storm that forced us to bed down in the negative-three-star Goat Hotel. So the road wasn't flooded, but the rain just kept falling and falling and falling. I had been caught in the rain many times before (riding a mountain bike, hiking, or camping), so I understood how the rain had the potential to intensify things. If it rains on your way into the mall, it's a mild inconvenience; if you get caught in the rain out in the middle of nowhere, it can turn fairly serious in a hurry.

Previous rains in Mongolia had pounded me for forty-five minutes to an hour, and then it was quickly replaced by the sun.

Not this time.

The first morning I noticed it was clouding up, I adjusted my layers, put my rain jacket in my backpack, and ran in tights instead of shorts and a long-sleeve shirt. I hit the road to heavy fog that turned into a mist and then a drizzle; the temperature dropped from the usual 90s to the 50s. After that drizzle, the rain never let up, though it would occasionally intensify to a shower that soaked me to the bone.

Halfway through my miles that day, I got into the support vehicle to eat a lunch of a peanut-butter-and-Nutella on flatbread made the night before, and then I would drink some Gatorade™ or SporTea™ (who were kind enough to sponsor me). I changed into some dry layers, thinking the rain couldn't last much longer because it had never gone on long before, and I set off into the rain again in wet shoes and socks because I didn't see the point of changing them.

I endured another fifteen miles soaking wet, and I was none the worse for wear by the time I got into camp that night. I knew setting up camp was a challenge for the team, so I felt bad for them, especially for my family. Nevertheless, all was well that ended well, so I hung up my wet gear, filled my stomach, and crawled into a dry sleeping bag to read *Fellowship of the Ring* by the light of a headlamp.

It rained all night, which is actually a very peaceful and relaxing sound if you are in a good tent, so I slept great that first night. But when I woke up, it was still raining. I had one or two dry layers I could put on, but because it was so damp and cold, the layers I had worn the previous day had not dried out overnight.

Back on the road again that morning, I was soaked again within the first hour of running—even the best gear in the world isn't proof against the steady pounding of Mother Nature. However, I wasn't too concerned because the temperatures weren't that bad. Again, I thought more of Lissa having to take down our tent and pack up camp in the rain, which is tough. I kept thinking that the rain couldn't last that much longer, but it did.

I had now gone through all my dry layers, so everything was either soaking wet in my bag or trying to dry while hung up wherever we could stretch a cord. At night, I started laying wet layers over my chest or legs while in my sleeping bag hoping that my body heat would help drive the wet out.

Ever had to dry out wet clothes by sleeping in them? Imagine pulling damp bed sheets out of the washing machine and making your bed, then climbing under the covers and trying to get a good night's sleep. Try to get any sleep at all! To further enhance the experience, set your room temp for forty-nine degrees, sleep on the hard floor, and replace your pillow with a rolled up hoodie. Do that every night for almost two weeks, and you begin to get the idea. (Running thirty miles before bed and running another thirty the next day is optional).

It made for very damp and miserable sleeping. And it worked just enough so that the next morning my wet layers were only damp, not soaking. The only thing dry I had to put on were the fresh pairs of socks from my sponsor Right Socks™. Thank God for small gifts (which I protected like Gollum guarding his "precious").

Day after day, I put on cold, damp underwear, damp tights, a damp shirt, and a damp rain jacket. If anything, after the third day, the rain *picked up* in intensity! And by the fourth day or so, I felt like I had a fever. *Oh great*, I thought, *I've pushed myself too hard, and now I'm sick.* I definitely did feel worn down, but otherwise I didn't *feel* sick, so I didn't want to tell Lissa because I did not want to scare or concern her. The fever stayed with me all night, and I didn't get cold, even though that night temperatures were in the 40s (which is one reason my gear wasn't drying). I reasoned that maybe my body was trying to compensate for the prolonged exposure to the hypothermia potential, so my internal thermostat had cranked itself up a few degrees.

One of the unfortunate things about being on such a tight schedule while running across the country is that you don't get to take sick days. I finally did tell Lissa, and she took my temperature 102 degrees. I tried some Tylenol™, and that brought the fever down, but then I felt cold. On the theory that my body was trying to compensate for the wet and cold, I quit taking the Tylenol and simply ran with a fever. I was continually wet, day after day, only getting to put on dry clothes in our tent.

A huge tribute to Lissa—against all odds and every effort of the weather, she kept our sleeping bags surprisingly dry for a long time, so we had a refuge from the rain. Moisture slowly invaded our gear, but we knew that if we had to sleep in wet sleeping bags, morale would plummet. But despite Lissa's best efforts, six days in, our sleeping bags started to get pretty damp.

Then the wind began to pick up, and one night even though we were lying right next to each other, I had to shout so the kids could hear me read our book. Somehow in the middle of the Mongolian plains, we were getting hit with a monsoon!

While running through that, even though my feet were soaked, I tried to avoid puddles because I didn't know what was in them. Like some sort of crazed, wet dancer slogging through the sugarplum fairy land, I traipsed along the road, dancing over puddles and trying not to sink down to my knee in the deep ones. I tried to close my jacket up and just listen to my music, mentally pulling myself into some sort of inner happy place.

On several occasions, I felt like I almost had an out-of-body experience. Conditions were so bad outside and I was so miserable that I would withdraw to such a deep place internally that I felt like a spectator to what was happening. It was like I was watching a movie with full digital surround sound authentically replicating the pounding rain on the hood of a jacket—my jacket! I could see my arms moving and legs pumping in my peripheral vision, but I was no longer concerned about balance or stride or avoiding puddles; I was just an observer trapped in a running machine.

I can remember running for hours in this trancelike state, my mind drifting and wandering through the library of my memory. Rows and rows of books held different memories, and I can remember reaching up to pull certain books off the shelf and relive a memory. I let the machine run and worry about stride and not twisting an ankle and staying hydrated and all the rest.

At times I felt like a passenger sitting shotgun on a long road trip. I would sit there with my head leaning on the window, watching the scenery float by. Too uncomfortable to sleep, too tired to engage with reality, I hovered in this dreamlike state. The machine of my body kept running, but my mind and my spirit drifted through a surreal dreamland.

It was a very weird, but this surreal experience seemed to help me get through the misery of all those miles in the rain—an escape mechanism from the aches and pains and constant, soaking wetness.

It was actually almost difficult to come back to reality, and at the end of the day when I would sit down to eat, I had to work to not simply let the machine shovel food into its mouth robotically. I had to "come down" and tune in to the people around me, laughing and talking. It took a conscious choice to come back to reality and be *present*. And with presence came incredibly sore muscles made worse by the damp, exhaustion, and wet.

Similarly, I understand the fight to be "present" as a father; it's easy to float through family times by being on your phone or to just tagalong on family outings. Sure, we might be there in body, but are we really *present*? Are we engaged? I tried to keep in mind that the sum of many little, ordinary moments add up to an extraordinary impact on a child's life.

Miraculously, the rain finally ended on one of our rest days—after *nine* days, which felt more like eternity in some soggy hell. We all came out of our tents like prairie dogs emerging from their burrows, testing the air with upturned noses to see if it still smelled like rain. The sun seemed like a long-lost friend, and we simply spent the day luxuriating in its rays and trying to dry out all our gear—and ourselves. An expedition of human prunes finally got to dry out, happy to not have mildew or trench rot and to have survived the great Mongolian Monsoon.

MANDATORY FUN DAYS

Plenty of people familiar with exploration know the name Sir

Ernest Shackleton. One of the heroes of explorers everywhere for his miraculous trips and Arctic expedition on the ship Endurance, Shackleton is probably best known for leading his problem-plagued expedition safely off Antarctica after their ship was caught and crushed in sea ice in 1915.

Lesser well-known is that while Shackleton was trapped on the ice with his men, once a week he would host talent shows as a way of boosting morale and building team cohesion. So while the climate was anything but Antarctica, I received inspiration from Shackleton's idea to institute Mandatory Fun Day for our expedition across the Mongolian steppes.

I would run for six days, but on the seventh day I would take a rest day. After the evening meal on the seventh day, we did a talent show with mandatory attendance. Selah and Kai would help Duya clean all the dishes and take down the tables in our large meeting tent. Then they would scurry off to our Fortress of Solitude to change into their "cleanest clothes"—because one should never go to a fancy function in dirty clothes. One of our team members would set up a big light in the tent that bounced off the ceiling creating a delightful ambience. Everybody had to bring something to contribute to the show, and this goofy idea ended up being great. (I say *everybody*, but EK, being so stoic and reserved, counted just by *showing up*.) The kids really carried the talent shows with multiple skits that they had all week to work on. Every show ended with a rousing chorus of "You Are My Sunshine" that Lissa led with her guitar. Then the lights would go out, and we would all melt into our tents, trying not to think about another week of toil and pain that would soon begin.

The next day all the goodwill and entertainment from the talent show was forgotten, and I was back to being a merciless taskmaster. But for one day a week, we all had something to help us decompress, and the other six days we all had something to look forward to.

LIFE ON THE STEPPES

Mongolia is a little smaller than Alaska, but it has about three million people compared to less than a million in our largest state. This means that there are more than twice the people per square mile as Alaska, but it sure didn't feel like it! Because of the vast horizons, it felt like we were alone on the steppe sea.

However, as remote and lightly populated as Mongolia is, we actually had periodic visitors who were out in the middle of nowhere, just like us. They would typically come riding up on horseback or on little Chinese motorcycles, and we loved these visits because people were always very friendly and curious about what the crazy Americans were doing.

Mongolia's rugged individualism, which is necessary to live a nomadic lifestyle out on the inhospitable steppes, also means that because conditions are so harsh, whenever you meet other people hospitality is super important. Conversation, which flowed through our translators, always went through a pattern that hasn't changed much for thousands of years. There's a greeting, and then they would ask where we were going, where we had come from, and how the weather was there. They would ask about the road and terrain we had covered, and then someone from our camp would always ask the same questions back. This would let us know the conditions ahead of us, which prior to weather satellites was the only way to know what conditions were like.

Visitors always engaged in trade—often simply the trading of information back and forth. Customary questions included how their health was, the health of their family, and the health of their *livestock*. Another strong commodity are stories, often about the winter and more about livestock.

Another custom was to offer the visitor a bowl of yak tea, which is made of yak milk and dark tea leaves, all heavily salted and completely foreign and unusual to an American palate. Whenever a visitor came to our camp, no matter what our cook was doing, she would stop to make this tea and some sort of snack. Visitors would always gladly accept these offerings, which can be very important because, in Mongolia, you don't know how long it has been since your guest has been warm or had something to eat.

Conversation inevitably turned to what we were doing, and no one could believe it. Every guest would ask our interpreters some variation of, "Why isn't he on a horse? Can't he ride a horse or motorcycle?" Probably under their breath they would then mutter something more direct like, "Crazy American."

SUMS

When we would come into little settlements, the people often received us quite differently. Most people were out grazing their livestock in the countryside, so the few left in these little *sums* were there for some reason or another, and often they seemed distrustful of visitors or maybe foreigners. They were reserved and cautious. We saw more of the stereotypical xenophobic Mongolian in these little settlements, but out in the countryside, people were more curious and open to conversation.

However, these little sums often had something that brought me back to my childhood of watching *Little House on the Prairie*—a general store where the locals bought basically everything they needed to survive on the steppes. Prepackaged Russian and Chinese junk food abounded, and two places outside the capital even had electricity and the occasional cold, carbonated drink in a refrigerator—a rare and precious commodity.

We normally are strong believers of keeping caffeine out of the hands of our children, but while in Mongolia, we couldn't resist the taste of home that even a warm Coke offered. Every American traveling abroad knows the joy of the universal constant, Coca-Cola™ and the small taste of home it offers. We all cherished the sugar rush of drinking the Coke and snacking on these Russian chocolate cookies. I especially liked a drink called aloe water that was simply water with chunks of aloe vera, and my body seemed to love it.

It was nice to have something to look forward to, so these little general stores were like vacation outposts along the route. We would encounter one about once a week or so at the pace of a man running across Mongolia, so they were real treats.

The only problem was that because the rest of the team was often ahead of me in the support vehicles, they would get into these settlements long before I did, eat their treats, drink their Cokes, and be sitting in the shade enjoying their sugar rush when I finally dragged myself into town.

So by the time I finally got there, they were rested, refreshed, and ready to go. But all I wanted to do was sit in the shade and drink my aloe water. Some variation of this conversation would almost always happen:

"Off we go; see you in five miles!"

To which I would reply, "But I just got here!"

I felt like little orphan Oliver coveting their scraps and perhaps finishing whatever few sips of their drinks might be left before I had to soldier on the five miles to the sport vehicle. This prompted another "conversation," where, as the mature leader of this expedition, I had to put my foot down and say, "Don't go into town without *me*! I want to enjoy it too!"

Despite my frustration, this rarely happened…

THE CHILDREN OF MONGOLIA

Another highlight of visiting these little settlements was meeting the children. They were always relentlessly curious. They wanted to touch our kids, and they would always want to come up to me and touch me—especially my gear. I ran with a bandana tucked under my hat to protect my ears and neck, doing my best Lawrence of Arabia impression, so the kids were always curious about that, my running shoes, and my GPS watch. After only five or six days, the summer sun had tanned me to almost the same color as the kids, but my scruffy facial hair stood out, as few Mongolians can grow facial hair. Lissa and Selah's long blonde hair also would attract awe and wonder.

I was surprised how even small groups of teenage Mongolian girls would come up to me because of the impression of innocence that they still had, like what we would expect from a seven or eight-year-old. Eyes full of curiosity, their innocence was refreshing in a jaded world.

Whenever we got to interact with the kids, we got out our soccer ball, and if the stop was long enough, we would have an impromptu soccer game. These stops were some of the highlights of the trip for us.

DANGERS ON THE ROAD

Besides keeping an eye open for thieves and pickpockets while in Ulaanbaatar, we didn't encounter many dangers on the journey. And while not officially a *danger*, what we called "squatty potties" definitely counted as a hazard along our route. From the time we left Ulaanbaatar till the time we got back, we didn't encounter a single flushing toilet. Bathrooms were more accurately called outhouses, and these little three-sided shacks with a board over a gaping hole were the most horrible places we encountered.

Counterintuitive to what we know in the states, where we look forward to a stop for a chance to use the bathroom, in Mongolia it was just the opposite. We dreaded having to do our business in the slums we visited. It was far better to take care of nature's call out in the middle of nowhere because the horrific smell from those squatty potties seemed to cling to the inside of our nose for hours after we used them.

While we didn't have to worry about bandits or robbers, the biggest danger we faced was actually alcoholism. In Mongolia, apparently the alcoholism rate is close to 80 percent, and a great many men we encountered out in these small settlements were drunk. Most of them were harmless, but we definitely needed to look out for the younger men.

One time, two guys rode up on a motorcycle and invited themselves into our meeting tent to sit down and visit. Tulga talked to them for awhile, and since I had gotten done with my miles that day, I was resting in my tent. I heard them talking, and after nearly an hour, they still hadn't left. This was a little unusual, so I pulled myself out of my sleeping bag and went to check it out. They were quite drunk, and Tulga was trying to politely get them to leave, but they were not catching his drift. In very broken English, they welcomed me to Mongolia and apologized for being drunk. Tired and grumpy, I told them that it wasn't okay to be drunk in our camp—that it was shameful and that they needed to leave. I'm not sure what Tulga said, but they were a little perturbed that the hospitality was over and they had to go on their way. We briefly wondered if they would come back to make trouble that night, but thankfully they didn't.

Another time I felt like I had a very close call. I had run through a small settlement, and I noticed six young Mongolian men eyeballing me. The support vehicle had already gone through town and was waiting for me miles down the road, and as I ran through by myself, I noticed these guys giving me funny looks. As I left the tiny town and headed back in the countryside, I could hear their motorcycles fire up and head my direction.

By this time in the trip, we'd been through so much that I wasn't scared, but I did wonder if I would have to go into Jason Bourne mode! They buzzed by me on their motorcycles, six guys on three bikes, and hollered something in Mongolian. I decided to give them the benefit of the doubt and imagine that they were cheering me on.

They stopped their motorcycles on the side of the road up ahead of me so I would have to run past them. As I got close, they started saying, "Hey! Hey!" and gestured for me to stop. I didn't stop; I just waved in a friendly fashion and kept on going. So they fired up their bikes again and kept pace with me, trying to talk with me. They were all roaring drunk at 10:30 in the morning! When they boxed me in with motorcycles to either side and another in front, I did start to get worried.

They seemed to want to talk, and I remembered thinking that as drunk as they were, I could probably shove them over and they would fall like dominoes, but what would that get me? There was nowhere to run to, nowhere to go. So instead of pulling out my moves, I tried to explain to them that I was running across their country. I managed to make out something like, "That's crazy!" in reply, and then they pulled out a two-liter bottle of warm, cheap Mongolian beer and offered me some. I told them I was running and couldn't drink, so they passed it around amongst themselves, guzzling that warm, cheap beer before stuffing it back in a jacket pocket.

So I waved and smiled again and pushed my way through them, got back on the road and resumed my run. Shortly after that, I heard them fire up their motorcycles yet again, just slowly cruising along behind me. I could just barely see them in my peripheral vision, and I was starting to get more nervous.

Just as they started to pull up on me, I crested a gentle rise and saw that about a quarter of a mile ahead were the support vehicles! I waved down to them and then turned to my new "friends" and told with words and gestures, "There's my team. Those are my support vehicles."

The little Mongolian motorcycle gang did a quick one-eighty maneuver and headed back to their town, leaving me to wonder what would've happened if the support vehicles hadn't been right there. I ran with two cans of pepper spray, but I was ready to use a Jedi mind trick first. With a swipe of my hand, I'd say, "This is not the runner you are looking for." Luckily, I didn't have to use either.

MORE DOGSSS

One of the few dangers besides the risk of injury that I encountered in Mongolia were the dogs. They were actually why I had the pepper spray in the first place. There were a lot of them, and other than superficially, they are not much like our faithful American house pets. Dogs in Mongolia fall into two categories: vicious and out to get you, or incredibly happy to see you. And you never knew which.

I remember one time seeing a particular dog on the horizon and being nervous. I got my can of pepper spray ready just in case, but this particular dog wasn't of the vicious variety. Instead, he trotted alongside me for miles.

Now you have to understand how lonely it can be out there. When this dog started running alongside me, I thought, *This little guy knows what I'm doing, and somehow, someway he must've known that I was lonely and needed this company.* He soldiered on with me for a few miles, helping me bear the burden of God's call to run across Mongolia. (Melodramatic, I know, but this is just where your head is at when you are in the middle of nowhere and are deprived of human companionship.)

Other times, I pulled out my pepper spray, popped off the safety, and started getting myself in a downwind position so I wouldn't get any back in my face. If there were more than one, they would get in a loose perimeter around me about eight feet out, barking and growling and working instinctively as a pack. One would press in a little bit, and I would turn to face it. As I did so, one behind me would move up as the one in front withdrew. I felt like Frodo being menaced by a pack of bloodthirsty Orcs.

Some variation of this may have happened a dozen times, and I quickly learned the phrase in Mongolian, "Oh-quee!" Loosely translated, it means "don't push," but it is the equivalent of us yelling, "Hey!" So I would shout in Mongolian (because that's what Mongolian dogs understand), and I was ready with my pepper spray. I also learned that if I picked up a rock to throw at them, they would back off.

Ultimately, I didn't actually ever have to use my pepper spray. It's really a minor miracle in and of itself that I didn't have to spray anyone or anything and that I didn't get bitten by any wild Mongolian dogs and need a month's worth of rabies shots.

THE BIGGEST DANGER

Earlier I mentioned that alcoholism was perhaps the biggest danger we faced, and I told you about the visitors we had. But I didn't tell you about how it affected the traffic. Traffic in Mongolia is bad enough because of the conditions, but judging by the innumerable multitude of empty vodka bottles by the sides of the road, people there drink and drive like people in America sip a cup of coffee on the way to work and think nothing of it.

In the states, cars look out for pedestrians. In Mongolia, it's the opposite. As a pedestrian, I lived in constant fear of cars. Only a small percentage of the roads in Mongolia are paved, those around the capital city, and pedestrians are so rare that drivers have no knowledge of yielding to pedestrians. It was their lane, their road, and they were taking all that they wanted to. Even paved roads had no shoulder, so any time a car passed, I had to jump into a ditch to avoid getting flattened.

I ran facing traffic so that I could see cars coming, and I learned that if I saw a car coming from a long ways off, I could run farther and farther out into the middle lane, which would urge them over. But even though there was no oncoming traffic for as far as you could see, Mongolian drivers do not like to cross into the other lane. So we would play this bizarre game of chicken, and at the last moment, I would jump back to the side of the road to create my own safety zone. Sometimes that worked; sometimes it didn't. Most frightening was the rare occurrence when there was a car going the opposite direction in each lane or when one passed the slower-moving vehicle right next to me. At the end of my miles on pavement, I felt like I could run ten extra miles just because of the stress.

CHAPTER 17

THE BEST AND WORST MEAL OF MY LIFE

Come what may, all bad fortune is to be conquered by endurance.

– Virgil

We were finally drawing near Ulaanbaatar, about two days out as the tired guy runs. I was on paved roads for the first time in I didn't even know how long, which was a different kind of scary because of traffic. We were close enough that Venus's wife and daughter even came out to visit our camp, which was fun. But I had no real concept of how close we actually were to the capital, so for me it still felt like miles and miles and days and days away.

The morale of the Mongolian members of our team was now running very high because they knew how close they were to being home. Plus, we would be taking a few days off while in Ulaanbaatar to visit the children at the dumps, so our Mongolian team members were in for a little break before we headed for the eastern border. Everyone was laughing and joking (except for EK, who was an ever-so-slightly-more-energetic version of his reserved self). After weeks and weeks of difficulties, toil, and hardship, fighting the elements, and just the daily grind, the expedition now had a lighter air as we reached the distant outskirts of Ulaanbaatar.

Mongolia only has a few hundred kilometers of paved roads on either side of the capital, which account for all the paved roads in the country, so we knew we were getting close when we hit blacktop—my nemesis, the Black Dragon. Other than the blacktop, the biggest thing I noticed was that, as we got closer to the capital, I was dodging fewer four-wheel-drive vehicles and more cars. Cars can't get too far out of the city, so like a sailor spotting seagulls and knowing land is nearby, I knew we were getting close.

The last rest day before we arrived in Ulaanbaatar, Tulga told us that he and the other Mongolians wanted to treat us to an authentic meal for dinner. My mouth said, "Great! That's wonderful!" but my mind was thinking, *What are we getting ourselves into?*

We soon found out it involved a sheep, and I had already had enough of Mongolia's uniquely flavored sheep to last a lifetime. Duya was very excited to make us this dinner, and she told us all about how she would prepare the sheep. We would eat the ribs together with potatoes and carrots; she was sending into Ulaanbaatar for the vegetables. Not only that, they would prepare it right there in front of us.

That was great, except that we just really wanted to rest and maybe find a stream to do bag laundry or take a bath. We had been on the road for well over a month and a half, so we cherished any chance we had to rest.

As the afternoon wore on, I didn't see that Duya was getting started on the meal, so I asked her about it. "Oh, they're bringing the sheep tonight," she told me.

"They're bringing the sheep *here*?"

"Oh, yes. This is a very authentic meal," she told me and then explained that, in fact, they would be butchering the sheep right there! *Great . . .*

Sure enough, Tulga's brother arrived from the city in a really nice Toyota Land Cruiser . . . with a live sheep tied up in the back of it. The two brothers pulled the sheep out of the back of the Toyota and were ready to butcher it—right there in the middle of camp! I immediately began to argue with them; I'm no expert, but I know that butchering an animal involves a lot of blood and other things. Things we didn't want in our camp.

"No, no," they told me. "There's no blood!"

"There's always blood when you butcher an animal," I responded. "You can't do it right here."

But they kept arguing with me as the American mindset clashed with the Mongolian way. Meanwhile, my daughter was busy petting the sheep we were about to eat. "Selah," I told her, "don't pet the sheep—that's dinner!" Lissa tried to comfort her as the fact settled home, but she got really upset.

We obviously didn't let her watch as they butchered the sheep in a truly unique fashion. Basically, they reached up inside and stopped its heart. Without getting into details, the sheep expired quickly and pretty humanely, appearing to have simply gone to sleep—sure enough, with almost no blood!

As I watched, I felt almost hypnotized. Tulga and his brother quickly dressed the sheep carcass, carefully packaging up the guts into a garbage bag to be taken well outside of camp. I was amazed how cleanly they were able to do it with almost no blood. Nevertheless, by the time they were done, the sun was going down, and we were all starving. We had had a small lunch in anticipation of this big, authentic Mongolian dinner. We were ready to end our day, but they were just now getting ready to start cooking.

Duya started boiling various sheep parts while the Mongolian men huddled over the sheep's head with a blowtorch, burning the fur off so they could right away eat "delicacies" that I won't get into. These "delicacies" were their favorite part, so I wasn't going to deprive them of even a single bite!

When the meal was ready, Duya presented us with sheep ribs that were more gristle than meat, measly potatoes, and pathetic little carrots. But she was overflowing with such joy that we couldn't help but try it for her sake. Unfortunately, the meat had a flavor something like sage that we associated with the particular odor of entering a family's gerr tent. As far as we were concerned, this is the smell of Mongolia, and it is not appetizing.

We didn't want to be rude, but the gerr-mutton was especially pungent, and after as few bites as possible to appease our excited Mongolian friends and show our appreciation, we excused ourselves to our tent. Our family had our own meal of six stockpiled Snickers™ bars and a jar of peanut butter for dinner! As we settled down for the night, we heard the Mongolians up and chatting and laughing late into the night as they enjoyed their authentic meal, which the silly Americans did not find pleasant at all.

BATTLING THE BLACK DRAGON

Having never driven into the city before, I had little concept of how slowly we were going. If we had made the drive before, we would've noticed that our pace was a snail's crawl, and it would've been mentally agonizing. After running on primitive two-track roads for so long, running along the side of the highway was intimidating because of the speed of the traffic. Out in the countryside there was some variation as the road went up and over rises or around various things, but this was straight as an arrow and boring (other than the constant danger of being flattened into road kill).

The entire country of Mongolia is changing, being dragged into the modern world by forces stronger than the native wild horses. The paved road is one of the biggest indicators of progress, and it is constantly expanding in Mongolia. Roadways will soon connect the entire country. In many ways, they are skipping straight from the horse to the automobile, completely missing the railroad stage that stitched America together. Regarding technology, they are jumping instantly from word of mouth between nomadic travelers conveying road conditions and weather to iPhones and satellites offering instant communication and information.

All of the little communities we saw while trekking across the country were only loosely connected by dirt tracks, but connect them with paved roads, offer them cell phones, and soon the entire country will change. We felt that by taking the time to run across the entire country, we were able to see this rapidly approaching change at a macro level from west to east.

The pavement I was running on served as a reminder of the expanding change that will overtake Mongolia. I could feel the forces of modernism in the heat radiating off the black asphalt, making me feel like I was running in an oven. The surface temperature over the asphalt was well over 100 degrees, with the general air temperature in the high 80s and 90s—a dry heat, though.

I called it Riding the Black Dragon. It was a battle between me and the heat and traffic. I had to do battle with the Black Dragon for many days as we drew closer to the capital (and later as we left it again). The settlements grew closer together, the traffic worsened, but I cowboy-ed up because I was looking forward to our time in Ulaanbaatar. Not only would I get a short break from running, we would spend time with the people we were there to help—the kids.

It made fighting the Black Dragon worth it.

BACK IN ULAANBAATAR

One day outside Ulaanbaatar, we camped in some fairgrounds used for festivals. We have pictures of men in what appeared to be speedos and long sleeve shirts from what's called the Nadaam Festival, a summer event Mongolians really enjoy. The games were long over by the time we arrived, so we had multiple square miles of flat, open parade grounds to ourselves.

No matter how close I sensed we were to the city, I dreaded asking Tulga how many days out we were because I didn't want to hear him say that we had three or four days left. But the morning after we camped at the fairgrounds, Tulga said over breakfast, "Today is the day you run into Ulaanbaatar!" Excitement abounded.

It was raining a little, which always slowed us down, but I knew we were within striking distance. We were close enough that Tulga's cell phone worked, and he received a phone call from the same TV station that did a brief interview with us when we started running, and now they wanted to come check in with us as we ran into the city.

Running into Ulaanbaatar was surreal. I had been there twice already: once way back in April when I flew in for a reconnaissance mission, and the second time when we landed in July to start the expedition. I remembered that I had thought then that the next time I came into the city it would be on my own power rather than by jet.

Also, coming into Ulaanbaatar meant that we had already covered about a thousand miles! It was a completely unbelievable distance for guy who had never run much more than a marathon ever, yet here we were.

I wanted to come into the city as the champion of Mongolia, to have the city roll out a red carpet and throw down palm fronds to celebrate my entry and this historic accomplishment. But in reality it was just a busy, bustling city that would just as soon run me over as give me the time of day. I was quickly humbled by the fact that I was just one small pedestrian in a very large metropolitan city, and that all the good I was trying to do for these children was just a tiny portion of what they needed.

I had to decide that if no one in Mongolia knew my face or what I was trying to do, it was enough that *God* knew. It was enough that some kids received help, that we made even a small difference. Running in to Ulaanbaatar was a little bit of an ego check. Yes, we had made it a great distance. Yes, we had raised money to help orphaned children. But we still had a long way to go, and the children had much further to go before they would have humane care. What we were doing was just the start.

I remember standing on a hillside overlooking the city and thinking, *Here I am, Ulaanbaatar.*

The city didn't care.

But God did. I was okay with that.

GRADING YOURSELF ON A CURVE

Mongolian hotels aren't picky about who they'll take. None of them are five-star vacation destinations for the famous, but we did have reservations at the Best Western™ Ulaanbaatar. After saying our goodbyes, we sent our Mongolian friends off to their families, their own beds, and a break of a few days. Venus helped us unload our gear and then tore out of there, headed for home.

We walked into the hotel excited like kids on the last day of school. The intense pressure required to maintain concentration and focus over such a great distance suddenly wasn't necessary, and we felt we could exhale, take a deep breath, and relax. We'd be taking a two-day break in a luxurious, by our standards, accommodation.

We walked into the lobby of the Best Western™ and saw the Ritz Carlton™! It was a nice hotel by Mongolian standards, but by the standards of having been on the road for upwards of forty days, it was positively marvelous.

While we waited in line with several other people in the hotel lobby, we felt out of place.

"What is that smell?" Lissa asked.

It took us a little while to realize what it was . . . some of the guests. Somebody smelled really bad.

It was us.

Until we had gotten into this clean environment, we didn't realize how dirty and smelly we really were. It made a huge impression on Lissa that we tend to grade ourselves on a curve when we examine our lives. Meaning, we tend to find people or situations that are worse than ours and say, "At least I'm not as bad as that." But then, among all these relatively clean people and in this clean environment, we were faced with the undeniable reality of exactly how dirty and filthy we were.

We got upstairs to our room, hauling all of our bags with us. As the expedition leader, I declared that Lissa was to get the first shower. It was a really interesting shower because it was in a corner and looked like some type of swanky time machine. The glass was tinted, so it was a little dark inside, but then a little dome light came on. Instead of a simple faucet head to turn it on and off or adjust the temperature, it had a whole bunch of different buttons and options. We could change the color of the lights, and we could adjust the water so it pulsed or streamed or jetted. Not only that, the water would either come out of the shower head like you'd expect, or it could dribble down from the ceiling of the little shower capsule. We called it the Disco Shower—some very impressive Korean technology!

Lissa disappeared into the Disco Shower for about forty-five minutes. When she finally got out, she said that she had spent about thirty minutes of that time just crying. "I'm not even sure why," she told me.

The whole experience had just been so overwhelming, we didn't know what to do with it. During the trip, the need for survival kept us full of tension and wound up, unable to come down. Something as boring and familiar as a shower had simply relaxed her defenses and allowed the tension to slough off.

We threw the kids in the shower next, and over the course of an hour, they drained the hotel hot water supply as they washed away a thousand miles of Mongolian dirt. We finally had to drag them out, which was a change from before the trip having to drag them *into* the shower.

Finally, after about two hours watching other people scrub off the grime, I had a chance to get clean and wash the dust (and worse) off. I felt like the water not only was cleaning the outside of my body but was also washing away the pressure of the expedition—to perform, to protect, and to lead the team. The trauma of staying wound up, perpetually on guard, had left me drained. Like a soldier coming back from combat, the relief of no longer being shot at for the first time in weeks was palpable, and I could finally let my guard down.

However much I got to relax, though, a tiny thought in the back of my head recognized that I was only two thirds of the way there. It had taken so much effort to get spun up to the level necessary to cross the first thousand miles, I didn't want to lose that. So in some ways, I let the attention and awareness necessary for being out on the open road wash away, but I did not let go of the mental toughness and preparedness I knew I would need to finish the job.

I was so tired. It was tempting to just completely let go; I really wanted to lay down that burden. But I knew that if I did, I would never be able to run the remaining 500 miles to the border, lead the expedition, take care of my family, and stay focused on the job that I came to do.

Before I stepped out of the shower, I made a conscious decision to not let the hot water and small comforts of this of modern convenience make me soft or cause me to lose sight of the goal. I would stay focused.

The job wasn't done yet.

A WELL-EARNED MEAL

We had each saved one clean outfit for the day we arrived in the city. After we got clean, we changed and headed downstairs. Even though we had eaten that day, something about relaxing in a hot shower had made us all hungry. We were now able to turn our attention to other areas of need, and we recognized that we were ravenous.

The hotel had a bar where you could order food, so we grabbed a table and found that ham and pineapple pizza was on the menu—my favorite! We ordered four different pizzas—one of everything because we just couldn't decide—and dug into the food. I had forgotten how much I loved melted cheese! Everything tasted amazing because of what we had been through and what we had been eating for so long. For Mongolian bar/hotel restaurant food, it was actually pretty good. The radio happened to be playing Bob Marley, so we sat back, stuffed ourselves with pizza, and listened to Bob Marley sing about life being good. It was the best meal of my life.

In that moment, life was amazing. We had made it to Ulaanbaatar safe and sound, we were together, we hadn't needed a medic, and we were all in one piece. We still had 500 miles to go, but we were two-thirds of the way there and had proven we could do it. We had endured forty-three days without a shower and sleeping in a tent. We traveled 1,000 miles over dusty, pothole-riddled, two-track roads. We had faced down dangers and persevered through trials. We survived miserable plagues of mosquitoes and spiders. We forded swollen rivers. We suffered through blazing heat.

So we laughed . . . we laughed a lot. We laughed at me because of how I looked as I hobbled around camp. We laughed at Selah and Kai as they wrestled EVERY night in the tent. We laughed at Lissa because she would ask in sheer amazement at least a dozen times a day, "*This* is the main road?" We laughed, as we had every day, at the insanity of the whole overwhelming experience.

It was a moment of pure bliss that I will never ever forget.

Oddly enough, our room had four beds. We had all been sleeping together for so long that at first we all tried to fit into a single bed. Finally, I realized that this was a little bit ridiculous, and we disbursed to our own beds. It was glorious to put our feet in clean sheets instead of a dirty sleeping bag. We had a great night's sleep.

In the morning, after a huge breakfast, we met up with a man named Baska. He would take us to the dump to see the children. My run so far had just been the vehicle, just a trapping. For all the focus it required to do it, now was the real time to get down to business.

It was time to meet the children at the dump.

CHAPTER 18

THE LOST CHILDREN OF MONGOLIA

The meaning of life is to find your gift.
The purpose of life is to give that gift away.

– Pablo Picasso

Not everyone has forgotten about the lost children of Mongolia who live in the dumps of Ulaanbaatar. For example, Baska was one who ran a feeding program and doing what he could for orphaned children living at the city dump. Baska cared because he had once been one of those children. Growing up in the sewer systems beneath the city like the other orphans, Baska was lucky. Someone noticed that he could fight, and somehow this dubious distinction earned him a ticket out of hell.

We made arrangements for Baska to pick us up and take us to

the dump, where he fed the kids. His English was better than my Mongolian, which isn't saying much. We were supposed to have an interpreter, but we weren't able to make that happen. So we got into Baska's vehicle, and he drove us to the outskirts of the city into what is called the Gerr District. This is an area on the hillside outskirts of the capital. Occupied by people who have migrated from the countryside into the city, these people are trying to make a better life. But because they have no money, or because the gap is too far for them to cross between an urban lifestyle and the nomadic one they've known for thousands of years, many of them end up unable to make the transition. They collect in gerr communities with no electricity, running water, sewage, or government services just outside the city where they can look down from the hilltops and see the relatively modern capital.

Life is very difficult in the Gerr District, and the poverty is crippling. People have few prospects for improving their lives, but as bad as it is near the tents, things can get worse. The Gerr District butts right up against the city dumps. If you think things are bad in these tent cities, even those people have it good compared to the ones who live at the dump.

Baska drove us to the city dump, and though I had read about it and seen some pictures, I was completely unprepared for what I saw. For all of the miles of the run, I had in the back of my mind what we were doing and why we were there but especially who we were helping. But it didn't really sink in until I stood on a hill overlooking the city dump just exactly how horrible and desperate the lives are of the people who live there.

We had been to the Children's Place Mongolia Orphanage that we had partnered with, but we had not yet made it out to the dump. Any child at the dump would give anything in the world for the chance to go to the orphanage, but for many of them there is not even that modest hope.

The capital has five main landfills, and Baska brought us to the one where he tries to help children. He warned us that we may not be able to get out of the vehicle if it were too dangerous, so he would first get out and look around.

"Why is it so dangerous?" I asked.

With difficulty, he explained that this was the best place for the worst criminals to hang out—their refuge. The police won't even go to the dumps; it's just too dangerous. Though drugs aren't as rampant as one might think, alcohol and violence abound. It's the worst place full of the worst people.

I've been to landfills before, and at first glance, this landfill didn't look much different than many elsewhere. However, they don't cover over the trash; they just pile it on. Building materials and trash abound, but restaurants also dispose there so the organic smell of rotting food is really bad. Everything broken and discarded and forgotten is to be found at the landfill.

At this point, we still didn't quite understand. We didn't understand why Baska brought us to this horrible place. We had wanted to work with the children. We didn't really understand.

We were about to.

THIS IS WHERE THE KIDS ARE

So I tried to ask Baska why he had brought us here. I reminded him that we wanted to meet the kids.

He looked at me and said in broken English, "This is where the kids are."

We saw the children in the orphanage when we first arrived in Mongolia. Don't get me wrong, being in any orphanage must be incredibly difficult. However, there was a night-and-day difference between the well-kept children in the orphanage and the ragged, blank faced children that we found at the dump near Ulaanbaatar.

In our minds, we had the very unrealistic expectation that the children that we saw would resemble the children that we previously met at the orphanage—disadvantaged but somehow still a sanitized Western view of orphans. Nothing could be further from the truth.

We were in tears at the orphanage, Lissa especially. It's pretty awful to be all alone in the world with no parents. But nothing could prepare us for what we saw at the dump. At the orphanage, yes, the children had no parents, but you could see the workers genuinely had love in their hearts, and it was clean and safe. And the children at the orphanage were easy to love on because they actually know what love is.

The kids at the dump do not. It was like the switch somewhere inside of them had been flipped off, and they simply no longer had the ability to love or receive love or affection. It was more than a foreign concept to them: showing love was completely alien to their existence.

Our jaws dropped as we pulled around a hillside overlooking the dump and parked. Among the debris and rubble and garbage, with carrion birds circling overhead on updrafts from the rank smell of organic rot, there were people. The workers were sorting the trash, and people were going through the garbage that trucks had just dropped off, scavenging for anything useful or to eat.

Baska told us that there are several hundred people who live in this particular landfill. Of those, many of them are children.

"Why are the children living here?" I asked.

"They can't go anywhere else. If they go into the city," Baska explained, "they will be arrested. They may disappear and be picked up by sex traffickers, mining operations, or something else."

It's really bad when the safest place to be for a child is a dump infested with the worst criminals of the city. How tragic is that? How awful is it that this is the place that gives them the best access to food, that lets them hide from sex traffickers and forced labor?

This is where the children are.

It was really hard to stand on the hillside overlooking the dump and consider the plight of these children. We had read a little about it, and perhaps our minds grasped a tiny sliver of the reality we now faced.

Baska got out and look around, and satisfied that it was at least momentarily safe, we were able to get out of the vehicle and go down toward the dump. We could see structures that looked like places people slept, and we could see the people who lived there. Eyes were starting to rise towards us; hungry, hopeless faces turning dark, blank stares our direction. To help keep us safe, we could not bring food or anything else to the dump; that would be a good way to get assaulted. Instead, we told people where we would be the next day, a little fenced-off area where Baska has a type of soup kitchen.

When we first pulled up to the city dump, we were utterly amazed that people could live there. It didn't seem like humans were even there as we pulled up. Then, like some sort of twisted parody of reality or a movie, people began rising up from amid the trash. They looked like the trash in which they lived, like some sort of bizarre camouflage. Because of the violence, especially the children find their only marginal safety by hiding.

We'd only been there about ten minutes, but Baska suddenly said that we needed to leave. We were attracting too much attention, so we hurriedly got back in the vehicle and took off. That first visit we left the kids in the car outside the dump to help keep them safe, but we had left the windows cracked so they could get some air. Flies had swarmed into the car, and both kids were crying, covered in flies. My heart was sick as Lissa and I realized that's what these kids dealt with every day.

Our minds simply could not process the sights and smells that assaulted us. People talk about being overwhelmed, but I had no idea what overwhelmed meant until I saw this. My brain could literally not comprehend that these were people, children, living in this place.

THE REFUGE

Baska drove us out of the dump, around the backside of the hill in a roundabout way to get to a hill that separated the dump from the tent city. This is where he was borrowing a little piece of property. He had a large gerr with a kitchen set up in a fenced yard.

An old woman was there to cook food that Baska would bring her, and she made meals for the children. So we went from the dump over the hill and into a little refuge for the discarded children of Mongolia.

We had brought juice enriched with vitamins, crackers, and cookies to hand out to the kids, and as Baska's truck pulled down the dirt road to his property, children started coming out of the woodwork shouting his name. Cheering, they followed the truck to Baska's setup—here was a true champion of Mongolia!

Dozens and dozens of little urchin children greeted us as we got out of the truck, all under the age of twelve. Here they found a little respite from the incredibly harsh life in the dump, the only safety many of them were likely to find anywhere.

We played games with the kids while the others got ready to distribute the food we had brought, and then we spent a while handing out juice and crackers and trying to love on the kids. Baska told us some of their stories in his broken English. We heard stories of tragedy and woe, each one enough to make you cry, but the stories came so fast that we found ourselves mostly stunned.

Baska was really excited that we would come back the next day and pay for a meal to be cooked for the children, and we were happy to come back the next day. With the money we gave him, Baska had bought all of the ingredients to cook a big meal for the kids, and the word had spread that there was food! Something like 200 children came to his compound for what was probably the only real meal they would get that day or perhaps for many days!

It was like something out of *Lord of the Flies*. Simple things that I saw crystallized how hard life really is for these children. In this refuge, they were on their best behavior, but even here they bore the emotional scars of what they'd been through.

I watched as two boys played with an old, flat soccer ball. One boy kicked it so that it rolled to the feet of some girls who were sitting on a bench near the fence. One girl picked it up and put it on her lap. One of the boys ran up and demanded the ball back, but the girl wouldn't give it up. He screamed at her, and when she still wouldn't give it back, he drew back like a professional fighter and punched her. I've seen kids hit, but this was with skill born from practice—a real haymaker that knocked her over backwards off the bench. The boy picked up the ball and went back to playing with his friend.

The little girl was probably no more than seven or eight years old, and the blow had hit her cheek. She got up and dusted off her already dirty clothes and sat back down on the bench, holding her cheek. Her little friends, who were sitting right next to her, were completely indifferent to the situation. This was not the first time something like this had happened. This was life, and life goes on — for these kids, violence is just part of the deal.

I also noticed that an older boy, maybe in his early teens, snuck into the children's refuge by climbing over the fence, probably on the promise that food was being served. He broke off a branch of a bush growing near the edge of the property that I'd recognized as some kind of stinging nettle. When it had barely brushed up against my leg, it raised a welt and itchy stripe on my leg that burned like fire for about an hour. I barely brushed this plant, but this little boy was using the stick he'd broken off (which I guess he could grab by the stalk, which did not have the stinging leaves) as a whip. Brandishing it as a weapon, he was threatening children and swiping it across their legs if they didn't give him some of their juice or cookies. Some of the workers would yell at him to chase him away but did little else, and here even with our efforts to help, injustice still managed to get into the camp and cause pain. One little girl was crying as her skin swelled up from where the stinging nettles had hit her leg. Her leg was already weeping and bleeding.

The boy went unchecked, laughing at the misery of the poor, smaller children who either had to give in to his bullying or pay the price. About a dozen kids had found a bench to sit on and keep their little plate of food the cook had prepared. The boy snuck underneath the bench and just swiped his stinging nettle weapon across the backs of the kids all in a row! He took great delight in seeing that the children, one by one, jumped to their feet and hollered. One little boy got hit, immediately stood up and dropped his plate of food on the ground, and then instantly burst into tears, crumpling to the ground with his hands over his head.

I couldn't stand to watch anymore, so I went to this little boy to try to console him, but I soon found he simply didn't know how to respond to my attempts to comfort him. He couldn't receive it because no one had tried to comfort him recently, maybe ever. He simply didn't have the capacity to receive my love, and as I sat in the dirt with him, my hand on his shoulder, I hoped that somehow a little piece of the love inside me stuck to him.

YOU ARE MY HANDS

I remember quietly saying a little prayer like, "Lord, You've got to help these children! My heart is breaking, and I can't imagine how broken Your heart must be over this injustice and the wrong that is happening to each of these precious, innocent children. Please, somehow, someway, will You restore all that's been stolen from them?"

I felt in my heart an answer—He would. But in that moment, I also understood that we are His hands to deliver a message of hope.

This one isolated event brought home why we were doing all this. We are His hands and His voice to give others a message of hope and love. With all the injustice, with all the tragedy, with all the trauma that these little ones have endured so early in their lives, they need to know Someone loves them—that there is hope.

At one point my son, Kai, came up to me with tears in his eyes. Before I could ask him what was wrong, he tuned his leg and showed me a bright red stripe on his calf where the mean boy had whipped him with the stinging nettle. My heart suddenly flooded with emotions. I felt deep remorse that I had allowed my son to be hurt like that. I thought to myself, "If you are going to swipe anyone, swipe *me*, not Kai. He is innocent."

I also felt burning anger rise up in me, "How dare that bully pick on my son. I am going to teach that kid a lesson!" But before any words came out of my mouth, Kai looked at me and said,

"It's okay, Dad."

My heart melted. I understood what he meant with those three words. Kai was really saying, "It's okay—that boy has been hurt, and hurt people hurt people." He was also saying, "It's okay, I don't hold you responsible for what just happened to me." What words could I say in response?

I just scooped Kai up in my arms and held him tight for a moment. When I set him down, the tears were gone, and he was ready to get back to playing with the other kids.

After I had sat with the other little boy for a bit, I picked myself up out of the dirt, dusted myself off, and went hunting for that fourteen-year-old boy. I knew enough Mongolian from chasing away scary dogs to confront him and shout that he needed to go away. I made him throw his stinging nettle over the fence and then forced him to leave, walking him out the front gate.

While addressing his aggression and injustice, I couldn't help but think about what his own life had been like, and that he was only repeating what had been done to him and what he had seen time and time again. Even though he was older and now able to prey on smaller children, he was still just a child himself, hungry and abused. As much as I couldn't let his aggression stand, I was filled with compassion for these children and their plight, this kid included.

We were astounded how young the children were — I mean, little bitty. Skin and bones covered in trash, they came to Baska's little piece of land for some modest help, some small safety.

IT TAKES MORE THAN TEARS TO CHANGE THE WORLD

Too often we are quick to blame God for the bad things in this world and yet too slow to acknowledge him for all the good. People like to hold God responsible for the bad things, as though that proves that He doesn't care or doesn't exist. But it's a two-way street—if you're going to blame Him for the bad, you must be willing to give God credit for the good in the world. The Bible is not filled with stories of people who had easy, blessed lives. The Bible is His-story, God's autobiography and our source text for life here on earth.

No, the Bible isn't full of stories of how God's goodness prevented bad things from happening. It is full of His presence together with us when bad things were happening and the fulfillment of a promise: God with us, Emmanuel. Jesus came to fulfill hundreds of prophecies that God would not let separation from Him go on forever, that He had a plan.

That plan, our hope, was in the person of Jesus Christ. God demonstrated His goodness to us in this that Jesus died for us so that we could be restored to a relationship with God.

A passage in Romans asks how will people hear the good news if no one tells it to them?[18] That is why we have to be His hands and voice sharing His love to other people.

This is what Baska is doing for the forgotten children of Mongolia. We were honored to be able to use part of the money we raised to help him buy the property he was borrowing at the edge of the dump, pay for a large gerr tent to go on the property, and to pay the cook so that he can feed a warm meal to two hundred kids a day.

We keep track of what Baska is doing to learn if his business model can handle more funds, because managing a blessing requires stewardship. We understood that we couldn't just throw money at the problem and expect it to go away. These are real, live children with real, intimate problems that a simple donation won't fix.

It takes more than tears to change the world. We looked at those children, we saw their dirty faces, and we cried over their stories. But that's just the start—it can't end with tears. Tears that just roll down our cheeks and do not end with action from our hands are wasted. Hurting and broken people come in all shapes and sizes, halfway around the world in Mongolia and right in our backyards.

18   Romans 10:14

STORIES

"I was just like that boy," Baska told us. He was pointing at one of the little children in the refuge, born and raised at the dump. His parents were never on the scene. He had lived by digging through the garbage for food, and he hid to stay away from people who wanted to do him harm. Life had been really hard for Baska, but at an early age he learned to fight to defend himself .

He actually became a pretty good boxer and fighter, and one day a Christian man saw some potential in Baska and rescued him out of the dump, training him as a boxer. The very thing he had depended on as a tool for his survival became his way out and a means of success.

It's interesting how often God will use our tragedy and turn it into our story. Just like the Bible isn't full of bad things being averted; it is full of redemption stories from cover to cover. Over and over, God uses people despite the bad things that happen to them, even turning to good some of the greatest tragedies in their lives.

That's Baska's story as well. Rescued from the dump by a man who believed in him and saw something in him, the very thing that helped him survive became a tool for his success. He now has an apartment, is married, and has several children of his own. But he has also come full circle to where he started, so he can love and help children at the dump in which he grew up.

It's a dump full of stories of lives waiting to be changed, like that of a girl, who was maybe five or six, that we all saw while we were there. She had bright red abrasions on her cheek that hadn't even started to bruise yet but would soon discolor her cheek and eye. She wouldn't tell us how she got it, and if she were a child from America, you could possibly think that she had fallen on the playground or hurt herself jumping off the trampoline. It was tempting to think it was an accident with this little girl, too, but I knew in the pit of my stomach that it wasn't something as innocent as tripping or playing too roughly. This injury had come from someone else, either an older kid, or perhaps a relative acting out of his own brokenness.

We experienced other stories that second day, which included riding with Baska back to the dump and sneaking under the twelve-foot-tall barb wire fence. I felt like I was looking up at a fence from *Jurassic Park* or something; they had really gone all out on it, high and sturdy. But there was a well-worn path underneath the barbed wire in one section, and after our whole family passed underneath, Lissa and the kids decided to go back and stay with the vehicle.

The smell was overpowering as Baska and I walked deeper into the dump, straining our eyes looking for hiding people. As we searched for the children, I didn't see anybody at first, but as we got deeper, we could hear voices that seemed to come out of nowhere. Some called Baska's name, and I didn't notice the source of the voices until I looked very carefully and saw people simply lying there on the piles of garbage. They were well camouflaged because their clothes and faces were so dirty, blackened from the acrid smoke of burning garbage, that they blended perfectly with their environment.

Baska took me to meet several people, who just had come up out of the garbage to talk with him. Again, we didn't have a translator with us, but we spent about half an hour just moving among these people—adults and many children. They were simply trying to survive by living among the city's refuse, the things that the rest of society have decided to discard as unusable, no good, or not wanted. These people had been discarded as well, and they were trying to do their best to keep living in the only place they could.

Seeing it so closely impacted me deeply. I've traveled to a lot of different places around the world, even to Third World countries with severe poverty, but I have never, ever seen anything as desperate as the conditions that these children live in at the dump. Even stretching my imagination's limits, I couldn't have imagined how harsh the same place would be in the winter—the brutally cold Mongolian winter. Remember, this is the coldest capital city in the world where daytime highs in the winter can be -30 degrees Fahrenheit—and those are the highs! I couldn't understand how humans survived here in the winter at all.

But more than imagining what these conditions were like in the winter, I got a glimpse of how hard their lives really were when I looked in *their eyes*, not to the conditions in which they live, the rags they wore for clothes, how dirty they were, or the smell. Their eyes told the story of incomprehensible hardship, difficulty, and brutality, and I could see in the faces of even little children that they had already seen great horrors.

One little boy we saw kind of summed up what we encountered. Obviously a child with special needs, he had a very small, emaciated puppy in his arms. It seemed very incongruent for this child to have this puppy in a country where they treat their pets very differently than we do in the west. The children in this dump cannot feed themselves, so it is not reasonable that he could feed this puppy.

This boy had a mother, and they were both filthy, covered from head to toe with garbage. The mother had given her life to Jesus, and we were trying to speak with them through a translator. Baska had tried to help her several times to get away from the dump, and she had even received a gerr tent outside a dump to live in. But because of her inability to maintain it, it was quickly overrun by some alcoholic guy who kicked them out.

The little boy kept hugging the puppy and hugging Lissa. He knew of love because his mother had tried to love on him, but he had seen so much darkness. At times, he would take the puppy and throw it as far as he could! The puppy would cry out, and he would run to come pick it up, and pet it . . . before hitting it on the head viciously!

We were overwhelmed by their inability to know and show affection and love. This little boy would kiss his puppy one moment and be violent with it the next, strangling it before petting it some more. This is a microcosm for their existence.

Reduced to little more than animals, these children knew betrayal and violence and violation as a way of daily life. It was startling to see the contrast between these poor children and those at the orphanage.

Two other kids stand out in my memory. The older one looked to be about four, and he held his little sister's hand. She appeared to be about two, but that is to my western eyes. They were probably a couple years older than they looked to me. Because of malnutrition, they were so small. We watched them come from far away, navigating among cars and other obstacles. We kept expecting to see parents, but there were none.

They sat by themselves, and the older brother did seem to be trying to look out for his little sister. He pushed forward for food, and we watched as he got an extra package of crackers and immediately hid them. From his furtive movements, it was obvious that people often tried to take what little he did manage to find for him and his sister.

Our hearts broke over and over as we witnessed one scene after another of bitter, total poverty. The poor in the west have no idea how good they have it; what we were seeing was hardship on a different level.

One person from a local church made the difference in Baska's life by taking him out of that environment and putting him in a more positive one. It may seem odd to us that fighting was his way out, but by learning to box, he not only made a success of himself but now is helping many little kids who are just like him. The child with the stinging nettles, doing the only thing he knows how to do—hurt because he has been hurt—and Baska represent two different paths. One hurts out of his pain; the other helps because he escaped the pain.

The difference is that someone helped Baska get out. Immediate relief isn't enough. Our visit was less than the tip of the iceberg compared to the need there. What they need is ongoing restoration, not to be "fixed" but to be known and have someone think they are valuable enough to rescue.

It quickly became apparent to us that what we were doing was just the smallest sliver, that the only lasting impact is an ongoing one. Baska and others have done what they can, but we recognized that they need resources. The most basic ones are that the kids need a safe place to eat and sleep, somewhere they can go at night to be safe from all the two-legged predators of the dump.

We continue to work with Baska to find ways of making a difference that will be lasting, restorative instead of simply a short-term rescue. The last thing we want to do is ignorantly try to help in ways that make sense to our western minds but that can actually make things worse.

PRAY FOR GRACE TO DO A LITTLE BIT MORE

When we were done, we got in Baska's vehicle and he took us back to our hotel—a luxury hotel with running water, air conditioning, and soft, clean sheets. I was in a daze as I took another shower and then simply lay down. I couldn't get the images out of my mind, couldn't help but think that even in the rustic conditions we had during the run, we were living a life that any of the kids at the dump would have called opulent and luxurious (if anyone had bothered to teach them words for those concepts).

The next day, we would be leaving for the final stage of the run, heading toward the eastern border city of Choibalsan and then three more days to the border itself. We would endure obstacles along the road, I knew. But they were now in a context I had never had before, and I would not complain. If by some miracle my effort to endure hardship for a little while changes the lives of any of those little children, I would gladly run to the limits of my endurance day after day, and then I would pray for grace to do a little bit more.

CHAPTER 19

Hopping Into a Trash Compactor

If one could run without getting tired,
I don't think one would often want to do anything else.
– C.S. Lewis

We ended up staying in Ulaanbaatar an extra day, heading to the dump again. We let Selah and Kai meet some of the children from the dump, and while we were apprehensive at first about how that would go, Selah and Kai impressed us at how quickly they just jumped in. Kai threw a ball with the boys and played tag, and Selah traded braiding hair with the girls, just like girls in nearly any culture do without even thinking about it.

The fourth morning, we woke with a deep understanding of what we'd seen and why we'd fought a thousand miles across Mongolia. We had seen the true depth of need of these forgotten children, were confronted with how small a contribution we were really making, and were galvanized with grim determination to finish the course.

When we'd begun the run, we were full of both excitement and blissful ignorance. It had taken us some time to get into a rhythm, but once we had, things had gone well. As we packed up our gear that morning, it was difficult because we had already grown to like soft beds, warm showers, and solid meals again. But we were eager, in a way, to get back in that familiar rhythm and finish what we'd come to do. It wasn't the eagerness we'd felt before we really understood what we were getting into; it was a professional desire to finish a job, to make good on a commitment. We'd met the living, breathing reasons we were here. This was for the kids.

Even Selah and Kai had their game faces on. They were ready to get down to business. No one talked about quitting now; it just wasn't an option. But it was hard to leave the Best Western Ulaanbaatar's creature comforts. With renewed, stalwart conviction, we met up with our Mongolian team and prepared for the last few weeks' push to the eastern border with China.

DON'T LET THE FIRE DIE

Putting on my same old running shorts, t-shirt, vest, and sunglasses was achingly difficult. I felt like a soldier gearing up for battle after one too many close calls with a bullet; battle was familiar, like an old acquaintance, but not a good one.

I immediately tried to summon that drive and focus that I had decided not to release in the shower that first day back in civilization. I needed to re-stoke those fires of motivation, and I found myself growing more and more frustrated as I realized that I had let much of that fire, that determination I'd sworn to hold on to, die a death of dozens of slices . . . of pizza. I tried to find my own game face inside, but all I could think of was the hotel bar/restaurant's reggae music and pizza, the feel of clean sheets, hot water in the disco shower, and blessed air conditioning.

Why did you let yourself get so comfortable? I demanded of myself. *You should've stayed in the zone. Now it will be that much harder to get it back.*

I couldn't start running straight from the hotel because of the traffic, so we drove to the outskirts of Ulaanbaatar, and I felt unceremoniously dropped off at the side of the road like a banished pet. I eyed my old nemesis, the Black Dragon, stretching away east like an arrow pointing to the sunrise of "progress."

It was time to fight my war again; time for the final leg of the journey.

FRESH LEGS, FADING SUMMER

My body responded well to the rest. I had wondered how it would react, but the days off had rejuvenated me, and my legs felt fresh and strong. My mind and attitude hadn't adjusted yet, but my body was quicker and remembered its job.

The team also seemed recharged by the days off. We hadn't seen our Mongolian friends since they dropped us off, and we were joined by a stowaway—Duya's little three-year-old daughter, Azuka. We quickly gave her the nickname "Little Songbird" because she was always singing some happy little song in Mongolian as she helped her mom in the cooking tent. It was a precious soundtrack for this last leg, and it actually reminded me a bit of the Mongolian children we were there to help.

We started putting on miles, probably about twenty miles that first day. We camped our first night beneath this modern monument to Genghis Khan (which they pronounce with a *che* instead of a *geh*).

Rising fifty off the plain and fashioned entirely from shiny metal, it looks more like an Autobot Transformer than a monument. Kai and I secretly wished it would transform into a jet or something before our eyes. So we were looking up at a giant statue of "Chengis Khan" in a beautiful meadow that first night back at work.

Over a period of four days, without bothering to tell us, summer had snuck out the back door. Just east of the capital, we passed through a small mountain range, but the altitude wasn't the problem. Fall was here, and there was a dramatic change in the weather. The mornings were cool and crisp, and suddenly the days weren't getting more than mildly warm instead of blazing hot like they had been less than a week ago. This made my days running a little easier, but we started finding frost on our tents in the morning.

It was like someone had flipped a switch; summer didn't gradually change into fall; it plunged. Around us, the few trees in the mountains were obviously already changing color, and in Mongolia, fall is not a long season. Winter would be close behind, and we didn't want to get stuck here when it started to snow. For one thing, we didn't really have the gear for extreme cold, though we were ready with warm hats, jackets, and the rest because of the cool nights.

Suddenly, we felt a new pressure, a new race. We were now racing against the seasons as well.

LOST AGAIN . . . REALLY?

Whenever we approached the settlement, the support vehicles inevitably ended up arriving before I did. They would find the general store to enjoy some of what my military buddy Jeff Fox called "lickies and chewies." Very rarely, we found a weak Internet signal where we could get online to check Facebook™ and such. Mostly, the team would just sit and eat snacks and drink (typically warm) Coke.

We've gone over this problem before, but it didn't seem to change the fact that I was inevitably behind the curve, and everyone was ready to head out by the time I even arrived. They were trying to leave me out, but the importance of being included just didn't really connect. And the draw of even a modicum of civilization was simply too much for them to resist.

East of the capital, I tried to remind the team that if we were going into town, I wanted them to wait for me. The last "big" town between the capital and the border was Choibalsan in the Dornod Province. Finally, this time they actually waited for me just outside the city limits. I ran up to the support vehicle with a big smile on my face.

"Thanks for waiting! Let's find a little store together!" I said.

"Okay, great. We will go straight down the road and meet you in a little while." That sounded fine . . .

. . . until I got into town and quickly realized that even though they tried to wait just outside of town for me, there was actually still going to be a big gap between when they arrived at the general store and when I would actually get there.

We did it again. Once again, they would get there ahead of me, have fun without me, and be ready to go by the time I arrived. I was upset.

So I was already in a bad mood when I jogged into town and realized that this settlement was different than most. Other than Ulaanbaatar, invariably all these little settlements were just a collection of gerrs or buildings along the only road. Now, I was confronted by something new and unusual—a *fork* in the road. Let me tell you, when you don't have to make a choice like this for a thousand miles, it's strangely daunting.

I looked in both directions, expecting to see the support vehicles in the distance and therefore know which fork to take. But I suddenly realized that our Lexus looked just like every Toyota Land Cruiser that populated Mongolia. There it was, to the right; no, there it was, to the left. Our Russian van drove by, except it wasn't ours.

Oh boy . . .

Now I was starting to get really upset; not only had they forgotten about me, they had abandoned me there at the fork in the road with no way of knowing which way to go. I felt very vulnerable out there on the roadside, with only a little bit of food and water on my back. I had no money, little language skill, and was completely dependent on my team—my team that had deserted me.

I thought it over. I could explore down either fork of the road and look for them, but if I didn't find them, I'd have to go back and try the other side. That didn't sound too appealing. My other choice was to just sit down and wait. With the mood I was in, that option sounded better. I decided I would wait them out.

But when twenty minutes of this tactic didn't work, I decided, "Fine, I'm just going to go to the eastern border without them!" I picked the left fork and just started walking down the main street of this little frontier-looking town. I didn't see anybody from the team or our support vehicles, but I did see lots of busy people all looking at me in a funny way, because, well, you know, crazy American in running gear. The town was bigger than I thought it was, maybe fifteen thousand people (which seemed gigantic compared to the rest of the little settlements we had seen so far).

If the Russians ever tried to re-create an old, burned out town along Route 66, Choibalsan would be it. At one point, no doubt, Choibalsan had thrived, but the sun had set on this town's lifecycle many years ago, and now it was only a shell preserving an image of the Soviet Labor Movement. Russia had once subsidized infrastructure, like roads and streetlights, but when Russia pulled out, all the education, money, and support necessary for the upkeep the town disappeared and was never replaced. Now old, dilapidated Russian-government-style buildings look down on unkempt roads and burned out streetlights and stoplights. It's like a bizarre ghost town that somehow still has people in it.

I hadn't expected the town to be so large, so when I got to another intersection, I thought, *Oh boy, if I keep going, I'm really going to get lost.* Unsure of what to do, once again I decided to sit down and wait on a rock right near the intersection, so I could see the vehicles and hopefully spot one of our support vehicles. I probably waited an hour before Venus finally came rolling up, his window down.

"Hi, Brian," he greeted like it was no big deal!

"Hi, Brian?" I echoed back. *That's it?* I hopped in the support vehicle, and Venus drove me back over to where the rest of the team was waiting. Sure enough, they were sitting in the shade surrounded by empty Coke bottles and candy wrappers. Lissa jumped up when she saw me because she had been very concerned.

"I told them to wait for you!" she said.

When they had pulled into town, she had looked down for a moment and didn't notice the fork in the road, and Venus had not bothered to tell her. When she finally learned of this, she told him that they needed to wait for me, but Venus assured her I would somehow know where to go.

"No, no, it's fine. He'll know right where to go," he had told her.

"How is he supposed to know whether to go right or left?" she had asked him.

But Venus had assured her, "No, no. It's really obvious the main road goes this way, to the left."

Placated for the moment, Lissa had chosen to believe him. It was only after I didn't show up in a timely manner that she began to get worried and made Venus go out and look for me.

This brought up a potentially disastrous attitude I needed to address right away. I had to confront Tulga because what was no big deal to them was a huge deal to me. At vehicle speeds, making a mistake and having to backtrack takes just a few minutes; for me, it could take hours.

More than that, I knew from previous outings that we needed to ensure we kept things tight at the end of the trip. It was tempting to slack off because we were getting so close. At this point, we perhaps had just a few days to the border. Victory seemed sure; the finish line was almost within sight. But that can often be when something goes wrong. It wasn't enough to just address this with Venus; I needed to have a talk with Tulga. We'd had one earlier in the expedition, and I wasn't looking forward to addressing this with him, but it needed to be done.

CONFRONTING TULGA

You may remember that scene from the original *Star Wars* when they go down the trash chute and into the garbage compactor aboard the Death Star. It was a critical moment of crisis, and I thought of my confrontation with Tulga in the same terms—a pivotal crisis.

Only two weeks into the run, the storm began to brew between our fixer, Tulga, and me. He was a runner as well, and I actually invited him to join me as often as he liked. At first, I enjoyed the company. But slowly, subtly, I picked up on the vibe that he wasn't out there to run *with* me; it was like he was running *against* me, like somehow he was competing with me.

You might think that a little healthy competition would spur me on to do better, and for almost a week I was unable to put my finger on what was bothering me. I just got frustrated when he ran with me. I was doing more than twenty-five miles a day by this point, and he would join me for perhaps ten of those. We would start out together, but within a couple of miles he would pull ahead and leave me in the dust. This triggered the competitor in me, and I didn't want to push my pace to catch up with a runner who was only doing ten miles, so I would let him go and just didn't say anything.

One day, I asked him if he would just start his miles behind me. *Problem solved*, I thought. Nope. The only thing worse than having someone running off ahead of you is someone running behind you and giving you the feeling you're being chased. Even starting behind me, he would catch up and pass me. It started to drive me crazy! I spent many lonely hours on the road wondering why this made me so mad, and I tried to give him the benefit of the doubt that he simply loved to run and was just getting some exercise. But I had this gut feeling that he was trying to prove something.

This all came to a head one day when I confronted Tulga. It didn't go well. At one of the checkpoints where I met up with the support vehicle (after having been passed again), I told him how I felt.

"Look, I'm sure you don't mean anything by it, but I don't want you to run with me anymore," I told him. "Every day I'm out here, pushing my body and mind to the utmost limits, but I'm competing with myself and with 1,500 miles of road. But when you run with me, I feel like you're trying to compete with me. So I'm asking you to please not run near me anymore."

He didn't take it well. "This is a big country," he responded. "Why can't I run if I want to? There are plenty of miles out here for both of us. It's my country, I'm Mongolian, and I should be able to run if I want to. I'm not competing against you."

As he talked, I understood more about why I was feeling the way I was. Everyone on the expedition had a job. Duya's job was to cook. Venus's and EK's job was driving. Lissa's job was support, taking care of the kids, and looking after me. Tulga's job was logistics.

My job was *running*.

I felt like Tulga was trying to do my job. When he ran with me, I began to lose sight of my place on the team. I couldn't speak Mongolian, I couldn't plan the route, and I didn't know the country. Those things were his job; things only he could do.

I tried to explain this to him, but he wasn't having it. We had reached an impasse, and finally my frustration boiled over and I yelled at him to stop running with me before stalking off down the road. The next several days were very tense around our camp. It wasn't like we could go our separate ways to cool off. We all lived, ate, and spent all our time together as we crept across the vast wilderness.

It was here I discovered what discord does to a team. I soon found that we had lost momentum. All of our attention was on the problem, instead of the goal. And it eroded our confidence in one another.

TRASH COMPACTOR MOMENT

It was here I began to think of *Star Wars*, *Episode IV*. Han Solo and Luke Skywalker have just rescued Princess Leia, but now they are trapped with no way out of the detention level. An argument breaks out among them, and their forward momentum comes to a screeching halt. They forget about the goal (their escape) and the dangers around them, and they start criticizing each other and blaming one another for the situation. This is where Princess Leia, being a decisive leader, grabs a blaster and shoots a hole into the cover over a garbage chute. Leading the way, she dives through the hole to get away from the Storm Troopers, and everyone follows her, somewhat reluctantly.

This is the classic bad-to-worse situation. No longer being shot at, they find themselves in a massive trash compactor. They resume their argument until Luke is dragged underwater by some creature that manages to live there. They rescue him, but it is a momentary reprieve. The wall soon begins closing in to crush them alive.

There is a moment in the lifecycle of a team when individuals stop working with one another and can work against one another. However, sometimes crisis can cause individuals at odds to actually gel as a team. In fact, this usually happens during crises, and I have come to call these "Trash-Compactor Moments": As the walls begin closing in, the intergalactic heroes must put aside their differences to help one another and try to lift one another out of the twisting metal and garbage that threatens to crush them. Their newfound teamwork is a revelation.

Tulga and I were headed for our own Trash-Compactor Moment. Three uncomfortable days followed my confrontation with Tulga, and the lighthearted, adventurous spirit of our camp was replaced by a great cloud of tension. One evening, as our expedition was settling in for the night, we noticed a storm building in the west. The lightning was magnificent in front of the setting sun on the vast, barren wilderness. After checking the stakes on our tents, we headed to bed for the night.

I woke at about 2:00 a.m. as a massive rainstorm pummeled our camp. The wind was blowing so hard that it would temporarily flatten our four-season, expedition-style tent. The rain was driving so hard I thought it would rip through the rain fly over the tent.

Over the sounds of the storm, I heard an unnatural flapping sound from the meeting tent. I instantly recognized that the wind was ripping up the stakes one by one and was on the verge of flinging our meeting tent out into the storm. Despite being bone weary and aching horribly from running thirty miles that day, adrenaline surged through my body and gave me the strength to jump out of my sleeping bag, grab my rain gear, headlamp, and go out to battle the storm.

The rain stung my face, and even though the meeting tent was just several yards away, it was difficult to see in the heavy rain. It was like driving into a snowstorm with your high beams on. Shielding my face as best I could from the driving rain, I stumbled over to the meeting tent and ducked inside. I tried to quickly assess the situation and saw that several stakes had been pulled out of the ground, and one side of the tent was flailing in the wind. Our tables, chairs, and dishes had been tossed around and broken. It looked like a scene from some Wild West saloon fight.

I opened a supply box and found some cord and extra stakes. I quickly cut some extra lengths of cord and readied myself to go back out into the storm. "This is nuts," I said to myself. I grew up in the mountains of Colorado and Wyoming, backpacking and climbing in wild places, and while I have endured many storms, this was the most violent I had ever been in.

I stepped back into the fury of the storm. Trying to grab the flapping edge of the tent felt like wrestling a many-headed hydra. Fear began to seep into me, getting under my jacket along with the rain. No matter how I tried, I wasn't strong enough to pull the tent flap down and hold it long enough to drive in extra stakes. Additionally, as I was fighting the storm, I noticed other stakes beginning to rip out of the ground.

Well, this is it, I thought. *Here goes the meeting tent. I hope it doesn't take me with it.*

Just as I was about to give up, another pair of hands came out of the darkness to grab the tent. The rain was driving so hard, I couldn't even see who was crazy enough to be out there with me. I shouted over the wind and rain,

"Pull it down long enough for me to get a couple more stakes in the ground!"

My mysterious helper grabbed the stake loops in a death grip and held them still just long enough for me to drive a couple of new stakes into the ground. In just a few moments, we had the tent secured.

I looked up at last and saw that it was Tulga out there in the storm with me, standing over me and holding the tent with both hands. We were both soaked to the bone and covered in mud, looking like a pair of drowned rats.

Suddenly, he broke out in a huge smile, and I knew we were thinking exactly the same thing: *THIS IS ADVENTURE!*

He helped me to my feet, and we went back into the meeting tent, where we cleaned up as much of the damage as we could and made sure the tent was as secure as we could make it. The wind was too loud to carry on a conversation, but no words were necessary.

This was our Trash-Compactor Moment—a hellacious rainstorm crisis that caused the two of us to forget our conflict and refocus on the expedition. We never talked about that night and the rainstorm, but we also never fought over running again.

Conflict and strife cause division. Division is the combination of two words, "di" meaning two, and "vision" meaning, well, you get it. Division is a momentum killer because it causes people to take their focus off the greater goal.

FOOTLOOSE AND FANCY FREE?

I knew that the team was getting pretty loose and a little too comfortable and complacent as we wrapped up the expedition. They could sense that our adventure was coming to a close, and I could tell that they didn't have the same attention to detail and were not taking the same precautions. We had established patterns and routines to keep us all safe during the first part of the run, and those patterns had become inconsistent, if they were happening at all.

It was time to have another conversation with Tulga; I could only pray it went better than the last one. "Tulga, now more than ever, more than any other time during the trip, these last days are extra important. We have to be even more careful," I told him. "I've been in the mountains enough and undertaken enough trips to know that it's always coming down from the summit that you're most likely to have an accident."

I needed him to help make sure that the drivers were being very careful and measuring their mileage to our camping sites, not going too far. I also needed him to make sure the Duya was being very careful with meal preparation and properly cleaning up afterwards because we needed to avoid any food contamination.

So I went over all the details and adamantly warned Tulga about taking these last days too casually. I ended with saying, for the hundredth time, "We've got to keep it tight."

His response? "Why? What's the point? This expedition is over."

"It's exactly that mentality that will get somebody hurt. The moment you do that and let your guard down, that's when something will happen. We've been safe this whole time. I'm not going to jeopardize that in the final few days."

His response was very alarming to me because all it would take was one bad turn to color the whole expedition. I had been working to keep my family on their toes, but the Mongolians were his responsibility.

However, Tulga took this opportunity to vent some of his frustration with me about how much water the Americans were drinking and how it cost him excessive fuel to boil the water. Also, we had previously agreed to share the cost of our meeting tent, but now it was beat up and had a few holes in. It had held up well, all things considered, but now he didn't want to share that expense.

And he picked now to bring these things up! He really unloaded on me, and I thought the unprofessional manner just showed the toll the trip's stress had taken on us all. We exchanged heated words, but I had miles to do yet. In addition to covering more than a marathon every day, I felt like I now had to police my fixer and his team, an extra weight I didn't want to be carrying.

With the issue yet unresolved, I walked away from the conversation. Over the course of the next three days, Tulga was quiet. I gave daily pep talks to the entire team about keeping it tight until they watched us fly out of the country. I saw enough improvement from that to make me feel better, and pretty soon we were approaching the finish line. The last day was in sight, we were all in one piece, and now the expedition was nearly over. Now I just needed to stay strong to the finish.

CHAPTER 20

THE FINAL MILES

Strength doesn't come from what you can do. It comes from overcoming
ing
the things you once thought you couldn't.

– Rikki Rogers

The miles northeast of Choibalsan to the remote, far eastern border with China were through beautiful grassland steppes. The nights were getting progressively cooler and cooler, and during the last week we woke up to frozen water bottles every morning and ice on the tents that we had to knock off. Mornings were now very chilly, about 28 degrees Fahrenheit. The days warmed up to be in the 60s and 70s, which made for pleasant running.

I kept hoping for a last surge of energy to help propel me over the finish line—something extra for a sprint to the finish. Three days before the border, it didn't kick in. Two days before the border, nothing, and each day felt like every other day. Every mile was hard, getting up each morning was difficult, and the end seemed to be approaching at a snail's pace.

Talk at mealtimes still revolved around the same three things: food, weather, and the miles ahead. We may actually have avoided talking about the finish line because we knew that this amazing, once-in-a-lifetime journey was about to end.

It wasn't until our last night in camp, ten miles from the border, that I could sense our team relaxing. Talk shifted to getting back to pizza and reggae music at the Best Western Ulaanbaatar, returning to family, and taking hot showers.

The trip really was about to conclude. *We wouldn't jinx it by talking about it*, I told myself. You can relax . . .

THE LAST TEN MILES

That next morning I woke to the thought that I only had ten miles to do that day. I was still sore, still tired, and everything just hurt. I never got that surge of strength and endurance, that final sprint to the finish line that I thought I would get.

The ritual necessary for getting ready to run that day was the same as any other, so I dragged myself out of my sleeping bag, got dressed, and ate breakfast.

Time to start running, I thought. *It's just another day but with a bigger payoff at the end. Do the miles!*

I was still several miles from the border when I saw it in the far distance—the border checkpoint between Mongolia and China. I could practically smell the Chinese air from there!

In those final few miles, I had a sudden attack of introspection, my mind thinking back over the trip and all we'd been through. I reflected on what I had learned. As the machine pounded out those last few miles, the brain riding inside it considered how my family and I had accomplished what everyone told us was impossible. What did that make us? How did it change us to have done what could not be done?

I finally came to the conclusion that it made me a *dangerous* person.

THE FINAL STEPS

As I ran up to the border (okay, I kind of shuffled and trotted to the border), my family stretched a string decorated with prayer flags across for me to break. These flags, superficially like the Mongolian prayer flags they hang up on their shrines or that Buddhists use, actually had the prayers and well wishes of family and friends written on them. We had borrowed the idea but turned it into our own celebration, and as I ran to the little checkpoint, I broke the string and accomplished what so many people had prayed for and believed for along with us.

I gathered my family up in my arms, and we all dropped to our knees right there on the gravel road. We prayed to God and thanked Him for His help and for keeping us safe. We thanked Him for making the impossible, possible. I didn't shed any tears; I wasn't overcome with sudden emotion. But I was incredibly thankful that my family was there to experience this moment together with me, to share in the triumph.

We shook hands with some officials and received congratulations from the border patrol. Minimal formalities concluded, I shuffled over to one of our support vehicles, pulled my shoes off, and put on some flip-flops. I decided that I wasn't going to wear another pair of running shoes for a very long time!

Since I was only doing ten miles that day, we had left the camp set up. When we got back to camp, Tulga pulled out a NASCAR-sized bottle of champagne. We popped the cork, and it sailed high into the air . . . before coming right back down on top of Kai's head! We all enjoyed a good laugh and passed around little cups. We made toasts to a successful expedition and enjoyed our bubbly champagne for a few minutes.

True to form for the whole expedition, after this brief celebration it was back to work tearing down camp and packing up for the drive back to Choibalsan, where we had made arrangements to fly back to Ulaanbaatar.

Remember near the beginning of the book when I talked about how we sat on the floor around a paper map of Mongolia and spitballed the dates and estimates on how long it would take us to cross the country? We had put my finishing day as noon on September 19. Well, we came pretty close to our estimate . . .

I touched the eastern border of Mongolia at 11:45 a.m. on September 19th! Only God could have pulled off something like that. With all the delays, interruptions, and little variables, we finished up supernaturally on schedule.

After we said goodbye to our Mongolian team in Choibalsan, leaving them to drive the distance back to the city, we boarded a plane, and made the quick hop to the capital. It seemed anticlimactic to stay one night in Ulaanbaatar before getting on a plane and saying goodbye to Mongolia. No fanfare, no grand ceremony. We were simply done. But it had been a grand adventure, and once again we had faced death and lived to tell the tale.

Our there-and-back-again journey was at last over. Like Frodo and Sam in *The Lord of the Rings*, we had seen the mission through to its completion. Despite difficulties, we had overcome.

In Tolkien's masterpiece, *Return Of The King*, Bilbo Baggins concludes the memoirs of his odyssey with a poem that feels especially appropriate to me:

> The road goes ever on and on
> Out from where it began.
> Now far ahead the road has gone,
> Let other follow it who can!
> Let them a journey new begin,
> But I at last with weary feet
> Will turn towards the lighted inn,
> My evening-rest and sleep to meet.

HOMECOMING

Two day's worth of travel later, we landed in Chicago, where Lissa's mom and dad picked us up. They had taken us to the airport and sent us on our way, full of apprehension yet supportive. I'm sure in the back of their minds they were wondering, *What's this guy doing to my daughter and grandkids?* But they had been a great source of support. It was easy to see the relief they felt seeing us happy, healthy, and successful.

Money for the forgotten children of Mongolia had kept coming in while we were gone. We split it between the Children's Place Mongolia and helping Baska buy a piece of property right on the edge of the landfill. He continues to feed as many as 200 children a day.

After we returned, I also had the opportunity to do numerous TV interviews, webcast interviews, blogs, and articles in newspapers. Also, I was able to travel and speak about Mongolia and the plight of its children to receptive audiences. In fact, we felt God was urging us to share what we'd learned of the need there so strongly that we put our yes on the table to any speaking engagements offered to us.

And we did, even when it seemed to cost us literally everything we had (to the point we had to raid our daughter's savings account). But we kept saying yes, and God kept showing Himself faithful; and He didn't just provide us enough to pay her back but to humble us greatly, time and again.

CHAPTER 21

LIVE DANGEROUSLY

The world is a dangerous place to live; not because of the people who are evil, but because of the people who don't do anything about it.

— Albert Einstein

To this day, I'm still figuring out exactly what it means to be a dangerous person. During the course of doing the impossible, God showed us that any barriers or limitations that others (or our own fears and doubts) had placed in the way are nothing for Him to overcome. When you have seen God do the impossible through you, you realize there truly is nothing beyond Him.

When people are *dangerous*, that means they are somehow a threat. When I say that I became a *dangerous* person in Mongolia, what it means is that I am now a threat to the limitations anyone seeks to put on me. I am a threat to any force that tries to use failures or mistakes to impose limits or sanctions on what God can do in my life. I am a threat to the status quo, to the comfortable life of keeping up with the Joneses and striving for a bigger house, bigger car, and all the trappings that we so commonly connect with success.

I am a threat to anything that gets in the way of living to my fullest potential because that is when I am most alive and when I feel the deepest, greatest sense of satisfaction. I'm a threat to anything that threatens to keep me from fulfilling the purpose for which I was created. We were not created just to make a living, to scratch by, or to only be interested in ourselves. We were all created to make a difference on this planet, but many of us have lost sight of this quest for a purposeful life, and we have lost the element of danger that can make a radically obedient person *dangerous* in the kingdom of God.

"Once you know there is no limit on what God can do through you, you're dangerous!" Lissa said as we talked about what happened to our faith in Mongolia. "The sky is the limit!" Because I am a dreamer, this plays out in big-picture ideas. For her, this realization is more daily and practical. For example, at one point, we went without a traditional income for over eighteen months, and we had to trust God for every need.

Mongolia made us *dangerous* because when we got back, we realized that there was nothing that God could not do through us. It gave us a whole new understanding of a Scripture so often carelessly quoted: "I can do all things through Christ who strengthens me."[19] I'm not sure how often we threw around that incredible verse flippantly and without really any understanding of exactly how true it was.

We understand now.

"It's made me dangerous because I don't freak out wondering how

---

19   Philippians 4:13 NKJV

it's all going to come together," Lissa told me. "I just know He *is* going to make it work together."

Now when we have doubts, we feel like God's encouragement is quick to say, "Remember what I did in Mongolia? Remember the 1,500 miles? Remember all the hundreds of details I took care of? I was in that, and I am in this. I am the Lord of before, during, and after."

This makes me recall all the doubts and fears people had heaped on us, all the concerns we'd had in preparing for the trip, and all the bumps in the road posed by issues like my ankle and tooth. I thought about all the concerns that had nearly crippled me during the flight from Ulaanbaatar to Ulgee. We smashed right through *all of them*! My family and I have become *dangerous*.

We now see life differently. Other things that are "impossible" no longer seem unattainable. People who cannot be stopped are a *dangerous* people because no matter what they set their eyes on, they *truly* know that with God all things are possible. With a disciplined mind and a strong back, with determination, perseverance, support, and encouragement, there is nothing those people cannot accomplish.

CLOSER THAN YOU THINK

Everything we went through, everything we learned, and all the fears and adversities we faced and overcame showed me something surprising. We are all much closer to living a dangerous life than I once thought.

So what stands between you and becoming a truly dangerous person? One small step—you must dare to step out in faith and say YES to the plans God has in store. I maintain even after all we went through in Mongolia that emotionally and perhaps spiritually the most difficult thing we did was put our yes on the table there at Camille's

Sidewalk Café before we told a soul about Mongolia.

An old saying goes, "The years will teach you what the days will never know." I didn't understand the transformation happening to me, even as I finished the last ten miles of the run. But in the aftermath of my Mongolia, I can look back at the years and see how various factors contributed to making me the person God could use to accomplish this dream. From nurturing my adventurous spirit in the Rockies but not allowing it to be my answer, to honing my determination with mentors who demanded a lot of me, to surrendering my life to Christ and marrying a woman who would be totally committed to God, and so much more; He was shaping me. I didn't have to be an ultra-marathon man or a bleeding heart for the world's orphans for God to give me an assignment that the fear of the Lord would see through till the end.

So what is God shaping you for? What impossible dream might He have in store for you tomorrow for which He is preparing you *today*? Just like I didn't know that the work ethic I learned in construction would be necessary to keep going when I was exhausted on the steppes of Mongolia, you probably don't know what the difficult things you're currently going through are teaching you that will pay off in the future.

And I believe that you are closer to being *dangerous* than you think you are. In fact, you may only be one step away!

So when will you say yes to the Mongolia God has in store for you? You may not even know it at this point. But what you can do now, whatever stage of life you are in, is decide that when God calls you, you will answer yes.

If you are committed to doing whatever it takes to obey God, I can promise you this: *you will find out*. God promises, "If you are willing and obedient, you shall eat the good of the land."[20] When you look back from the other side of the impossible dream that God took years

20   Isaiah 1:19 NKJV

to prepare you for, you'll know how it all fit together for your good and how His plan for you took every event of your life and turned it for your good.

And when God has done the impossible in your life once, you'll know He can do it again. It's no longer a dream or wishful thinking that you can do all things through Christ who gives you strength.

It's reality.

JUST HOW WEAK I AM

If anything, crossing the finish line in Mongolia showed me how weak I really am. This may sound like an odd statement coming from someone who didn't have a running background and yet successfully ran fifty-seven consecutive marathons to become the first person to run across Mongolia. But it's true.

No one will ever really know the depths of my doubts, fears, and insecurities about this trip. Only God knows my heart, and I cried out to Him when the pain was unbearable. He is the one who knew how badly I wanted to quit, how lonely I felt out there on a dusty two-lane road that seemed to stretch into infinity. He was the one who supplied me with strength to carry on when I was ready to quit. He gave me the courage to get up every morning, despite my aches and pains. He supplied me with the compassion for the orphans of another country and inspired a method of easing their suffering just a little bit.

No, running across Mongolia showed me I am *weak*. It put God's strength and my weakness into stark contrast. It made it easy to make Him the one who gets credit for anything positive, inspiring, or admirable that my trek across Mongolia accomplished.

It showed me in no uncertain terms how *big* God really is. And let me tell you, He is really big! There were many times leading up to the trip that we ran into roadblocks, and just as we were about to give up or get stopped dead in our tracks, God made a way for us. Over and over, He made the way where there seemed to be no way. He orchestrated things better than the greatest symphony director could ever dream.

And in His sheer *bigness* and *goodness,* He showed me how far my strength could go before utter desperation allowed His grace to pick me up and eventually take me across the finish line. I learned how to grab hold of God's promises for my life by faith. He showed me with one step, by simply lifting my tired foot and putting it forward, that it only takes faith the size of a mustard seed for God's promises to release His grace into our lives so that we can accomplish what He has called us to do. No matter what He's dreaming up, His grace is sufficient for you.

This planet is covered in people who need God's grace every moment of every day. I got a real impression of how much He loves each and every one of us as I struggled to use running 1,500 miles to raise money for orphans most of the world has forgotten. I will always be amazed that God could stir the heart of this ski bum turned youth pastor to touch the lives of some children on the other side of the planet. He loves them so much that He sent a family from across the world to Asia, pulling them out of their jobs, orchestrating the impossible, and then guiding them across an entire country to demonstrate His great love for "forgotten" children and to show those kids that *He* had not forgotten about them.

Just thinking about that makes me more *dangerous.* I was just as surprised as anyone else that I actually made it across the finish line at the far eastern border with China. I hadn't expected this calling, but I discovered a new quality that had been placed in me as I accomplished it. I was now dangerous, not in the sense that I am unpredictable, violent, or unstable (but I have always been at least a little bit crazy), but in the sense that I had become *unstoppable*.

Lissa and I now recognize that there is no assignment from God that is too big for us. As long as God calls us to it, we know He will see us through it. And that confidence makes us indomitable. We know it's not about us; it's about His life flowing *through* us.

You might think this indomitable spirit could breed egotism, but if anything, we have never grown more in humility then we did by running across Mongolia. We came face-to-face with our weaknesses *and* His strength. There's nothing like seeing your failure meet God's strength to show you how small you are and how much you need God. When you are nothing but a colorful speck running across the vast Mongolian countryside, like a cork bobbing in the Pacific Ocean, you understand your place.

Our family got to see this firsthand, and I will always be grateful for my family trusting that I really had heard from God—enough to follow me halfway across the world. My amazing wife, Lissa, witnessed God's greatness right beside me, but she had to step out in faith in a completely different way to put her yes on the table that day at Camille's Sidewalk Café and commit to accomplishing whatever God called us to do. Everyone in our family made sacrifices to come be my support crew on this trip, and they not only did a fantastic job, I watched each one of them grow in amazing ways.

I started this book by talking about the fear of the Lord. More even than the precious children of the dumps of Ulaanbaatar, it was the fear of the Lord that inspired me to obey and do whatever God told me to do. He came first; they got to benefit from the obedience He called me to. Watching His plan unfold, I saw God's power, love, and grace in ways I've never experienced it before. His love for me and all the people on this planet, His patience and kindness, His grace, and His strength were on full display before, during, and after the trip. He brought me safely through this expedition, transformed me into a *dangerous* person, and blessed thousands of kids in the process. Just think what kind of God we serve to bring together such disparate pieces and players in order to accomplish such a wide variety of goals.

UNDER-QUALIFIED AND OVERWHELMED? NO

PROBLEM.

You've heard me refer to *The Lord of the Rings* over and over in this book, but let me tell you why I love it so much: I identify with it. The story features a small, insignificant hero assigned a task that seems insurmountable. The whole world is massive, dangerous, and out to get him. Success seems impossible. But he perseveres through incredible odds to accomplish something great, something that benefits the whole world.

What I love best is that this is exactly what God does with *every single one of us*: He sends seemingly insignificant and under-qualified people into the teeth of life to accomplish big dreams and impossible tasks, and then He brings them out the other side.

That was me. That was my Mongolia.

Every day, people are taking the first step toward the impossible with nothing more than faith and hope to guide them. My desire is that you recognize *you can be one of them*.

If you feel under-qualified and overwhelmed, know that you're not alone. If you haven't even identified what your "Mongolia" is yet, do not lose heart or become discouraged. Say yes to God.

Now.

Before you read the fine print.

Commit to following Him. Determine now that no matter what He calls you to do, you will obey, and watch as He puts a dream in your heart.

Whether or not you've defined the call God has on your life, you can say yes today. You can step out—*today*. It may be just the first step in a 1,500-mile journey, but it is *the most important step*. Trust Him to bring you through, one step at a time.

On the other side of your Mongolia, you will see the fulfillment of God's promises and plans for your life. You, too, will experience what it's like to smash through every opposition, to be indomitable and unstoppable. *Dangerous*.

You will know what it's like to be Strong to the Finish.

CPSIA information can be obtained
at www.ICGtesting.com
Printed in the USA
FFOW02n1030200618
47150029-49735FF